CULTURAL DEMENTIA

DAVID ANDRESS is Professor of Modern European History at the University of Portsmouth. He is the author of *The Terror: Civil War in the French Revolution, 1789: The Revolutions that Shook the World* and *Beating Napoleon.*

CULTURAL DEMENTIA

How the West has
lost its history and risks
losing everything else

DAVID ANDRESS

An Apollo Book

Typeset by Adrian McLaughlin

Printed and bound in Great Britain by
CPI Group (UK) Ltd, Croydon CR0 4YY

MIX
Paper from
responsible sources
FSC® C020471

Head of Zeus Ltd
First Floor East
5–8 Hardwick Street
London EC1R 4RG

WWW.HEADOFZEUS.COM

Contents

To Robert Andress

Introduction

This book argues that recent political events place the UK, France and the USA in a state of catastrophic cultural dementia. That is a very strong term, and I mean it absolutely seriously. It is not an image to be deployed lightly. My own father died of Alzheimer's in May 2015; most people's families now include at least one similar story of terrible decline. It is precisely because what confronts us now risks being an equally horrifying slide into dissolution that the term is warranted here. And because a culture, unlike an individual, may hope to recover from its dementia, before it is too late.

Our current dementia takes the form of particular kinds of forgetting, misremembering and mistaking the past. In that sense it is not nostalgia, which is at root merely a form of homesickness for the remembered past. Nor is it, any more than an individual's dementia, a simple matter of amnesia. In most cases, the amnesiac is aware that they do not remember; and knowledge of that lack – and of the potential to fill it from external information – is something to cling to. The dementia sufferer is denied the comfort of knowing they don't remember.

By disintegrating a person's coherent recollection of their personal history, dementia strips them of their anchorage in the past. Who they were and who they are become muddled; their own identity and those of their loved ones become confused and dissonant. Situations cease to make sense, erupting unexpectedly into a mind that thinks itself in another time or place and cannot hold itself lucidly in the present. Anger, bitterness and horror coexist with fond illusion and placid self-absorption. Practical action becomes impossible. For many, there is a lapse into hallucination, delusion and paranoid suspicion of all around them.[1]

Le Pen. Brexit. Trump. These might once have been the punchlines to a joke. But no more. The processes that have brought these names to global attention are nothing less than symptoms of rising cultural dementia. The former great powers of the historic 'West', now old in ways that cultures have seldom been before – *actually* old, demographically speaking, in previously unthinkable terms – seem to be abandoning the wisdom of maturity for senescent daydreams of recovered youth. Along the way they are stirring up old hatreds, giving disturbing voice to destructive rage and risking the collapse of their capacity for decisive, effective and just governance.

At the core of this is an abandonment of political attention to history, understood as a clear empirical grounding in how we reached our present condition. Historical stories abound; but as deployed in public debate they are often little better than dangerous fantasies, constantly at risk of abrupt and jarring collision with reality. Unlike Germany, for example, these countries have never undertaken the painful process of *Vergangenheitsbewältigung*: the coming to terms with the past that ceases to treat it as a comforting inspiration, and wrestles with the evils it conceals. Not even Germany, of course, has completed such a process irreversibly and entirely happily. Chancellor Merkel's noble decision to open the nation's borders to refugees in 2015 created a backlash that helped the anti-immigrant, conservative-nationalist Alternative für Deutschland party to a poll breakthrough in the 2017 Federal elections. However, as has been the case with many far-right movements across Europe, the AfD's 'breakthrough' only netted them one in every eight votes – well below the almost one in five shared by the major forces at the other end of the spectrum, Die Linke and Die Grünen.

The presence of groups such as the AfD is an unpleasant component of the 'new normal' of global politics, but so far has not produced any dangerously disruptive systematic consequences. Until these groups and their toxic messages are able to claim 30 per cent or more of the vote, we can still reasonably hope that the centre in Germany and elsewhere will hold. By the same token, looking further afield, the manipulation of democratic structures and aggressive chauvinism that Russia regularly deploys is, in the long term, more normal than not for a state that has struggled to tolerate a real civil society at any point in its history. Much like the ruthless control still exercised by the Chinese Communist Party, we can consider it to be deplorable but not catastrophic.

France, the UK and the USA, however, are supposedly the collective cradle of Western democracy, the nations that, quite literally, created the culture of codified constitutions and rights on which the Universal Declaration of Human Rights was based. Even if, as we shall see, such a self-image has often been little more than an illusion, it has been a uniquely powerful one – not least in fuelling unhesitating global military and political interventions by all three countries. The current condition of these nations, challenged by powerful bottom-up movements that question all their previously assumed values of openness, *does* have the potential to be uniquely catastrophic, at least for those of us trapped within these states if not more widely still. How any part of the world would sustain support for democracy if all five permanent members of the UN Security Council were to become open, convinced and militant chauvinists is a question that does not bear too much reflection.

Until recently, continued global economic and cultural leadership spared politicians in Washington, London and Paris from the need to confront where their national wealth came from, or how their languages came to dominate the world. Comforting illusions of progress concealed worsening symptoms of relative decline and internal divisions amounting to gross injustice. As economic progress has so visibly come to a halt in the past decade, stripping away that illusion of inexorable improvement, delusion has taken its place. Declarations that immigration can simply be halted, that long-dead industries can be restarted, that crumbling infrastructure can be replaced overnight, and a generous welfare state upheld and extended for the right sort of citizens, have abounded.

These claims, coming from the right and the far-right of the political spectrum, draw the natural condemnation of others further to the left. But it is important to recognise that this is not merely a continuation of old ideological struggles: these developments are even more dangerous because they are self-destructively mistaken. They are detached from the actual history of how our societies took on their current social, economic and cultural forms; and they are wrong about where those societies fit into the world around them. They make no more sense than a dementia sufferer demanding that his carers let him get the train to work in his pyjamas. Just as a confused eighty-year-old cannot bend the world to his perception, so a Brexiting Britain or 'Great Again' America cannot return old prosperity to their rustbelts by willing it to happen.

This dimension of sheer wish-fulfilment is often neglected in the anguished debates that have raged on the liberal left over what to do for, with or about the 'working class' that has voted for such things. A language that articulates 'legitimate concerns' about the negative impacts of immigration and globalisation has often resulted, while often neglecting the extent to which such concerns are rehashings of tabloid myths and undisguised racial prejudice. But whether or not the anxieties and desires of these groups are justified in anyone's eyes by their current experiences matters not at all. They are the deluded product of a detachment from historical context that renders them almost literally meaningless. Following through with these ideas will produce only an ever-accelerating spiral of crisis and suffering, even for those who support them most ardently.

From Shanghai, Mumbai or Mombasa, where the next century is being crafted, it might appear that none of this is relevant, except perhaps in the question of exactly how fast we may continue to slide from dominance to insignificance. But a world in which nuclear-armed powers stagger from one crisis to the next, fuelled by delusional bitterness, is not a safe world for anyone. Our urgent question is how we can escape our present confusion and reconnect with historical reality in a way that is tragically denied to individual sufferers of dementia, finding a new global role as cultures that embrace the realities of their long and complex pasts and refashion their heritage for the common good.

1
Roots of the Present Crisis

There is now a crippling void at the core of politics in the historically leading nations of the West, an absence of reflection so profound that it is hard for conventional commentary even to perceive it. In the former global powers of Britain and France, and the troubled superpower that is the USA, political perceptions are breaking dangerously free of a mooring in actual history. At the very time when shifting global power-structures – and the looming catastrophe of climate change – demand a confrontation with the realities of past and present, electorates and commentators are swerving around those realities, latching on to random distorted visions of the past in place of an undesirable future.

The roots of this problem run deep into history. In the summer of 1947, George Orwell identified some of them in a short essay entitled 'Toward European Unity'. Here he presented three bleak scenarios for the nuclear-armed future, one of which – eternal oligarchic stalemate – was the seed of *Nineteen Eighty-Four*. Against this gloom, he pressed the case that 'democratic Socialism must be made to work throughout some large area' in order to give the world an alternative, and that western Europe was the only suitable location to start.[1] Orwell acknowledged that 'the difficulties of bringing any such thing into being are enormous and terrifying', and went on to list four of them. Two were the essential opposition of both the USA and USSR, and one the then still hugely influential Catholic Church – a reminder of the widespread 'clerico-fascism' of the period and his own experiences in Spain. The fourth, to which he devoted almost as much space as these others combined, was the practice and legacy of imperialism.

In discussing this, Orwell voiced a basic historical truth that still haunts the West:

The European peoples, and especially the British, have long owed their high standard of life to direct or indirect exploitation of the coloured peoples. This relationship has never been made clear by official Socialist propaganda, and the British worker, instead of being told that, by world standards, he is living above his income, has been taught to think of himself as an overworked, down-trodden slave. To the masses everywhere 'Socialism' means, or at least is associated with, higher wages, shorter hours, better houses, all-round social insurance, etc. etc. But it is by no means certain that we can afford these things if we throw away the advantages we derive from colonial exploitation. However evenly the national income is divided up, if the income as a whole falls, the working-class standard of living must fall with it. At best there is liable to be a long and uncomfortable reconstruction period for which public opinion has nowhere been prepared.

Colonial territories, he argued, 'must cease to be colonies or semi-colonies and become autonomous republics on a complete equality with the European peoples' if a democratic Socialism was to have any chance. The difficulty of realising this vision – weeks before India's disastrous and hastily imposed Partition took effect – was clear, as was the underlying risk:

> the British worker, if he has been taught to think of Socialism in materialistic terms, may ultimately decide that it is better to remain an imperial power at the expense of playing second fiddle to America. In varying degrees all the European peoples, at any rate those who are to form part of the proposed union, will be faced with the same choice.

This prophetic voice from seventy years ago announces in a few short paragraphs both the failures of the intervening decades and the disastrous choices that voters, commentators and politicians appear to be making to avoid coming to terms with reality. Orwell's most gloomy prognostications did not come to pass, but neither did we manage to advance towards his beloved 'democratic Socialism'. The question of what would really happen if the West became equal with everywhere else was avoided. Instead, postwar generations were brought up to see generous welfare provision as a historic accomplishment of their national societies, belonging to them, along with a continued leading role in the world economy, as a birthright. From its origins this assumption held a dangerous tinge of racial privilege.

The long-term reality can be summed up in a few basic facts. India before British imperialism was a wealthy part of the world – indeed, this was a prime reason for the eagerness with which merchants flocked to its shores, to gather the high-quality manufactured goods that sold for premium prices to European elites. In the middle years of the eighteenth century, there was very little difference between the living standards of the average Indian and British worker.[2] Two hundred years later, at independence, the vast majority of the Indian population lived in a grinding poverty by then vanished from Britain. In 1960, per capita GDP in the UK was seventeen times greater than in India. By 1970, it was thirty-eight times greater; and by 2000 sixty-three times. But by 2015, it had fallen back to only twenty-seven times greater; and a year later, only twenty-three times.[3] Similar pictures could be painted of imperial and post-imperial relations all round the world. A great historical bubble is deflating, and it is as much about what happened 'after' empire as during the classic age of imperialism.

In the USA after 1945, the suburban 'American Dream' that had been interrupted by the Great Depression resumed its march. In the UK and France, nationalisations and public provision under the guidance of 'expert' planners marked out a different route to the same goals of present prosperity and future opportunity. A genuine focus on improving the lives of the core populations in these countries made the period between the later 1940s and the early 1970s into what the French label *les Trente Glorieuses* – thirty glorious years of well-planned growth. In comparison with the years that came afterwards, these decades saw a moderation of extreme wealth, and a rising share of real income for ordinary workers, which from our present vantage point, after the reversal of these trends, still looks to many like a golden age.

That view is only possible, of course, by closing one's eyes to some of what Orwell had already seen. Suburban America was a racially segregated landscape, with 'white flight' from urban areas refashioning the earlier 'Jim Crow' era of explicit discrimination. 'Sundown towns' that physically excluded non-whites could be found across the country, and the epic struggle for Civil Rights demonstrated by its extent and intensity – and terrible casualties – how the USA exercised an almost imperial domination over parts of its own population. That non-white part was also excluded, by countless subtle and overtly violent means, from much of the rising prosperity of the era, and has continued to be marginalised in geographic and social terms. The USA was formed as an empire, in its acquisition and rule over most of its current territory. Native American tribes and nations still live in complex and troublesome relationship with the states overlaid on their historic territories. Inhabitants of Guam and Puerto Rico live with most, but not all, the rights and representation of US citizens, as horrific neglect in the aftermath of 2017's Hurricane Maria has demonstrated.

In Britain after 1945, the Labour government may have hurried out of India, at the cost of 15 million dispossessed refugees and a million deaths, and abandoned its 'mandate' in Palestine to violent partition less than a year later, but it made very little progress otherwise towards decolonisation. Imperial territories were still seen uncontroversially as opportunities for Britons to exploit, even if under the banner of 'modernisation'. Labour ministers launched the infamous 'Groundnut scheme' to grow peanuts (primarily for processing into cooking oil) in what is now Tanzania. Tens of thousands of demobilised British soldiers volunteered to join the Groundnut Army and were shipped out to East Africa with the goal of clearing and cropping a vast 150,000-acre zone. Almost £50 million was poured in over four years, before the scheme was recognised as completely unviable and abandoned, having reduced the land it had cleared – less than a third of the original target – to a dustbowl.

Under the same Labour administration, settlement of white people in Kenya continued to be encouraged. The original imperial landowner class was joined by a wider range of middle-class professionals and businessmen and these, being less economically secure and more anxious about their status, would prove to be particularly aggressive as anti-colonial unrest became the Mau Mau Rebellion. Like the so-called 'Malayan Emergency' of the same era, straddling the boundary of Labour and Tory administrations, the first half of the 1950s was marked in Kenya by brutal insurgency and counterinsurgency. On the part of the rebels, a campaign of killing those they regarded as African collaborators was punctuated by the murder of several dozen whites, including women and children. The outraged colonial authorities imposed large-scale internment on groups suspected of rebel sympathies. Widespread torture in the form of prolonged beatings and physical mutilation led to the death of some 20,000 rebels, in addition to over 1,000 official executions. Local and imperial authorities had full knowledge of all these horrors, but colluded to hide them from public sight – except where rebel atrocities were used for propaganda.

Even within the Labour government, private prejudice about the colonies was rife. The Chancellor of the Exchequer, Hugh Dalton, wrote in his diary in February 1950 in horror at the idea of being posted to a governorship in West Africa, ruling over 'pullulating, poverty-stricken, diseased nigger communities, for whom one can do nothing in the short run', and who were 'querulous and ungrateful' for imperial efforts to raise them up.[4] Meanwhile in Britain itself, economic reconstruction drew in a steady flow of the 'West Indian' immigrants who first arrived in 1948 on the *Empire Windrush* and who, as they spread out beyond the port cities where ethnic mixing had been a fact of life for centuries, encountered persistent hostility. The racial dimension of that hostility was always clear.

Postwar Britain was so desperate for labour that workers were scooped in from the displaced populations of Eastern Europe, from Malta and Cyprus and in huge numbers from Ireland – by 1961, one in every six Irish citizens was working in Britain, some of them shipped over like so many cattle, with labels round their necks saying 'British Factories'.[5] On the *Windrush* itself were several dozen Polish women, collected from a curious wartime safe haven in Mexico. Probably the wives of Polish men already settled in Britain, they were all designated in documents as 'H.D.' – Household Domestic labour.[6] Most of these groups, which numbered many hundreds of thousands, were allowed to assimilate gently – after some early press grumbling about some of the Europeans being enemy aliens – and the huge disruption of the era faded from popular memory.

For the black population, things were different. Some 125,000 West Indians, and a little less than half that number from South Asia, had arrived by the late 1950s. With an economic downturn raising tensions across the workforce, a confluence of racial and sexual alarms among groups of young white men saw the alleged treatment of white women by black men used as a pretext for violent attacks on the latter.[7] 'Race riots' from this point on became a potential and actual threat to what politicians dubbed 'race relations': the management of tensions caused by the collision of endemic racism and casually laissez-faire immigration policies. 'Immigrant' and 'black' became implicitly linked in public attitudes. By the early 1960s, the postwar assumption that all races were citizens of the same empire and could move freely around it had been replaced by new distinctions of status for entry to the UK that, however muffled, were essentially racial. This was still far from enough for the swelling chorus of voices that Enoch Powell amplified in his infamous 1968 'Rivers of Blood' speech. Throughout this era, as internal turmoil grew, British troops continued to fight anticolonial rebellions in far corners of the world, from Cyprus to Yemen to Borneo.

France faced a parallel series of conflicts. The governments of the 'Fourth Republic' formed after the Liberation, as they carefully planned the economic renaissance of the battered Hexagon, had committed themselves to also delivering urban modernity to their colonial populations. While channelling notions of universal progress, this vision was also entirely dependent on those populations' willingness to remain subjected to Parisian dictates. In the late 1940s, France remodelled its empire into the 'French Union', a nominally constitutional and democratic global federation – but one in which non-white populations voted in 'electoral colleges' with less influence than whites. The real problem with the idea of guiding populations to higher levels of development was demonstrated by events that began on the very day that Nazi Germany surrendered: 8 May 1945. French troops opened fire on a victory parade in the Algerian town of Sétif in which banners demanding independence had been displayed. Attacks by local Algerians and the authorities escalated, with more than 100 white settlers being killed in nearby villages and a reprisal campaign that historians agree probably killed at least 6,000 Algerians in the following weeks.[8] At the same time, at the other end of the Mediterranean, French troops began a three-week campaign to suppress a movement for Syrian independence, killing hundreds and ending with a two-day artillery bombardment of the opposition forces clustered around the Damascus parliament building. While opinion in Metropolitan France barely noticed these events, they set the scene for the bitter struggles that followed.

By the end of 1946, France was openly at war with nationalist-communist forces in Indochina, culminating in 1954 with the expulsion of the French, after humiliating defeat by their former colonial subjects in full-scale battle at Dien Bien Phu. That same year, smouldering conflict across northern Africa ignited into sustained guerrilla warfare in Algeria, which was technically a fully incorporated region of France. This war cost France more than 25,000 military dead over the next seven years, alongside the loss of a larger number of Algerian auxiliaries, while they inflicted over 140,000 casualties on their enemies. As in Kenya, torture of suspects was normalised. A recent monumental study of these conflicts opens with the chilling juxtaposition of a young Algerian woman's account of physical and sexual torture and the memoirs of a French general, openly and unrepentantly recounting what had been done in the name of preserving empire. Both texts were published in France in 2001, and the second outsold the first.[9]

The war in Algeria ended only after it had destroyed the Fourth Republic itself. Faced with an attempted right-wing coup in favour of a hard line against independence, the Republic's leadership turned in 1958 to the wartime leader Charles de Gaulle (ironically viewed as a desirable figurehead by the coup plotters themselves). Building a highly presidential Fifth Republic around himself, De Gaulle used his moral authority to push through an independence settlement for Algeria over the next three years, at the cost of exposure thereafter to assassination attempts from recalcitrant right-wing settler groups.

Right up to the end of this process, violence, including bombings, had convulsed both Algeria and France. Extremely aggressive responses from the Parisian police, including a blanket curfew on the city's Algerian population, culminated in a mass attack on a demonstration of Algerian workers on 17 October 1961. Essentially given licence to kill, thousands of police shot, beat and threw protesters into the Seine, murdering possibly as many as several hundred. The full truth of these events was rigorously covered up by the authorities, gaining no public acknowledgement until the 1990s.

It is emblematic of the relationship between France's colonial and metropolitan political cultures that a much smaller (though still horrifying) incident of deadly violence, the killing of nine white trade unionists and communists at the Charonne metro station after a demonstration in February 1962, produced an immediate public outcry. A mass funeral procession of several hundred thousand people was held, with the full might of left-wing mobilisation, and the 'Massacre of Charonne' acquired a permanent place in the French left's litany of state crimes. The leader of the police responsible for both massacres, Maurice Papon, a close associate of De Gaulle, was later exposed as responsible for both the rounding-up of Jews in wartime Bordeaux and the torture of insurgents in 1950s Algeria.[10]

In these same years France caught up with where the UK had reached a decade earlier, and tested functional nuclear weapons – with supreme irony, in the Algerian desert that was just about to be surrendered. Both the UK and France, under governments of left and right, had pursued nuclear-power status since the late 1940s, and have of course retained it to this day. Anglo-French mushroom clouds in safely distant imperial territories bookended what was otherwise an era of visible decline. Sitting at its heart was the fiasco of Suez in 1956, a sorry tale of desperate collusion and half-baked military adventurism. Attempting to retake the nationalised Suez Canal from Egypt by force, before being obliged to withdraw under intense US pressure, marked the point at which, in practical terms, two centuries of global power began decisively to fade. The theoretical ability to kill millions was a very expensive and not-very-useful replacement for the practical ability to impose political solutions thousands of miles from London or Paris.

The difficulty of adapting to this new situation is ironically marked by the early years of resistance to nuclear weapons themselves. The Campaign for Nuclear Disarmament began life in Britain wedded to a rhetoric of global leadership – the very first Aldermaston march of 1958 had been literally under the banner of 'Britain Must Give the Lead'. 'Setting a moral example' was identified as a way for Britain to retain greatness without military dominance, and historic actions like ending the slave trade were explicitly cited as precedents. Time and again through the early 1960s, CND policy documents and public positions assumed that it was the responsibility of the UK to lead and direct resistance to the threat of atomic destruction. In the aftermath of the 1962 Cuban Missile Crisis, CND's newspaper *Sanity* opined that Britain had 'failed miserably' to demonstrate any continuing military greatness, 'But CND says there are other kinds of greatness. We have been pointing them out for a long time. Can we now start exploring them?'[11] It seems to have been an article of faith among the clerics, intellectuals and activists who took this highly oppositional position that it was, nonetheless, part and parcel of the special qualities of Britishness – and the British place in the world – to do so.

*

While CND positioned themselves instinctively at the moral forefront of progress, politicians did so with low cunning. Just as De Gaulle was bearing down on the Algerian War, Prime Minister Harold Macmillan signalled the abandonment of a decade of staunch Tory resistance to rapid decolonisation. In possibly his most famous utterance after 1959's claim that Britain had 'never had it so good', Macmillan told the South African parliament on 3 February 1960 that 'The wind of change is blowing through this continent. Whether we like it or not, this growth of national consciousness is a political fact.' In the face of rising unrest, political pressure in the United Nations and the possibility of generalised Soviet-backed anticolonial warfare, Macmillan's government had decided to cede independence as quickly as possible to whatever forces could be found willing to accept continued friendly relations. Pronouncing this in front of the stony-faced architects of Apartheid put Britain on the side of the angels, even if it was effectively an admission of defeat.

Harold Macmillan – almost a caricature of an ageing patrician, though his family's wealth actually came from the publishing business – also devoted considerable energy in these years to positioning the UK as Greece to America's Rome. Building a relationship with the thrusting young administration of John F. Kennedy, he hoped his avuncular charm could override a strong tendency in Washington to see Britain as a declining empire and awkwardly needy ally.[12] At the personal level this seemed to succeed, but did little to shift Kennedy's determination to aggressively resist communism – producing the failed Bay of Pigs invasion of Cuba, the brinkmanship of the 1962 Missile Crisis and the first steps towards deep entanglement in Vietnam.

By the early 1960s, as the first cohorts of the post-1945 'Baby Boom' came of age, the politics of the West seemed poised for a generational confrontation. For the Labour Party, looking to a shining future was the route out of 'thirteen wasted years' of 'Tory misrule', as well – not incidentally – as a deflection from damaging internal strife over nuclear arms. Thus the party's new leader, Harold Wilson, had many reasons to promise in September 1963 a 'new Britain' to be forged in the 'white heat' of a scientific and technological revolution. Insisting that 'there is no room for Luddites in the Socialist Party', he called on his comrades to wholeheartedly embrace change, denounced 'educational apartheid' in grammar schools and promised tens of thousands of new university places.[13] Through pages of detailed discussion about the potential for change in different sectors of the economy (written in full paragraphs, unlike modern political soundbite-speeches), Wilson proffered a vision that helped Labour overcome a Tory majority of almost 100 to scrape into power in 1964 and push ahead to a substantial 96-seat majority in the 1966 snap election.

Perhaps the most significant paragraph of the 'white heat' speech, in historical hindsight, is one near the beginning that takes a very different tone:

There is no more dangerous illusion than the comfortable doctrine that the world owes us a living. One of the dangers of the old-boy network approach to life is the thought that it is international, that whatever we do, whenever we run into trouble, we can always rely on a special relationship with someone or other to bail us out. From now on Britain will have just as much influence in the world as we can earn, as we can deserve. We have no accumulated reserves on which to live.[14]

When Wilson spoke those words, Macmillan's Tory government had already suffered the brutal rebuff of being vetoed by Charles de Gaulle from membership of the European Economic Community (EEC), as it then was. Four years later, at the end of November 1967, the French general would repeat the gesture against Wilson's own bid, rejecting the idea that Britain's maritime economy was compatible with the agricultural heartland of the then six-member grouping.[15] Only a week before this, the prime minister had been forced to decree a substantial devaluation of the pound, as exports struggled against dock strikes and the grim international impact of the dramatic 'Six-Day War' between Israel and its neighbours. The white heat of the technological revolution seemed little more than a flickering ember.[16] 'Swinging London' might have been in full flow for several years, and Beatlemania had conquered the world, but keeping the wider British economy alive was starting to become very difficult indeed.

Britain finally made it into the EEC in January 1973, with barely time to settle in to new arrangements before the entire West experienced the profoundly disorienting 'oil shock'. Petroleum-producing countries, with their non-white leaderships, flexed their economic muscles in disapproval of US support for Israel in the Yom Kippur War. While their outright embargo was short-lived, quadrupled wholesale prices became a new fact of life, as did rising inflation. *Les Trente Glorieuses* were over.

Underpinning this whole era had been the effort to retain the unfair advantage that Orwell had highlighted in 1947 and Wilson had counselled against in 1963. The immigration that so enflamed tensions was constantly spoken of in terms of 'labour shortages'; but, as with the huge influx of Asian workers to the textile towns of the north, it was just as often an attempt to find workers who would settle for wages low enough to keep British employers profitable. Much like immigrants of the twenty-first century who are found sleeping packed into garden sheds, such workers did not do this to themselves but rather were the prey of landlords and employers.[17]

At the global level, pursuit of economic advantage pushed British governments into a vacillating relationship with what had once been the empire and was now the Commonwealth. Throughout the decade of efforts to join the EEC, Britain played a weakening hand in trying to maintain some sense of preferential treatment by these territories as a trading partner while repeatedly prioritising the richer, nearer market of the Continent. Sentiment and economic sense interwove with a persistent belief in British entitlement to do well out of trade, even as its industrial infrastructure grew outdated through years of under-investment. Conservatives would come to blame over-mighty trades unions and increasing industrial strife for the besetting evils of 'stagflation' – and in the short term they won the argument, launching the country on the Thatcherite experiment. But this did not solve the underlying question of where an ageing post-imperial power fitted into the world.

This dilemma extended beyond the economic realm into the geopolitical, and rings down to the present day. In September 2015, History & Policy, a think-tank devoted to publicising the value of historical awareness for public decision-making, produced a paper highlighting the trap into which British defence and global policy-making was falling.[18] Faced with the political and practical impossibility of a major increase in military spending, the UK government risked failing to take the hard decisions that the Labour government of the 1960s had done in choosing to withdraw British forces from 'East of Suez' and focus on European NATO commitments – action that had allowed the UK to play a major role in the security of Europe until the collapse of the Soviet Bloc.

The afterlife of that investment was sufficient to carry British forces through participation in the subsequent 1991 Gulf War, peacekeeping in the Former Yugoslavia and other post-9/11 operations down to the 2014 withdrawal from active engagement in Afghanistan. Most of these more recent commitments, of course, had drawn the UK decisively East of Suez once more; and the decision to confirm that for the foreseeable future was marked in December 2014 by the announcement of a deal to create a base for the Royal Navy in Bahrain, independent of existing US facilities there.[19] Like so many geopolitical moves, this one tied the UK to a regime that had a very dubious human-rights record, having invited Saudi military intervention in 2011 to repress popular unrest and continuing to use torture to suppress dissent.[20]

What the History & Policy paper focused on, however, was the parallel with the 1960s situation, when post-imperial Britain had been simply incapable of maintaining its global posture without a ludicrous disengagement from the security of its neighbours, which remained critical to its own security and overlapped with the anxious bipartisan effort to join the EEC. Continuously trimming funding for all capabilities while aspiring to maintain them created a looming risk of systemic incapacity. The Wilson government's recognition of this dilemma saw them abandoning the aspiration to maintain a fully capable native aviation industry, and setting in train the end of the Royal Navy's aircraft-carrier fleet.

Almost half a century later, UK governments started with a much smaller military yet were making contradictory choices about it. Huge cuts to service personnel and front-line equipment had been made since the aftermath of the 2008 economic crisis, but at the same time government rhetoric – and decisions such as the completion of two new aircraft carriers – signalled a determination to project power globally. As the 2015 paper highlighted, the logic of this (and the only way to afford such spending in the medium term) was an eventual disengagement from the European defence sphere, if indeed 'the preeminent strategic threat' remained Islamic terrorism. But that would only be possible if 'Europe could divide responsibility for tackling the threats it faces between its member states taking account of their history and capabilities'. What effect a chaotic and bitter Brexit might have was not discussed, because of course in September 2015 such a thing seemed wildly improbable.

The France of the Fifth Republic pursued its own adventures in imperial continuity throughout the Cold

War decades, and beyond, while enjoying a semi-detached relationship with NATO that reflected De Gaulle's sense of national grandeur. Driven out of its biggest colonies, it converted some of its more scattered territories into integral parts of France – so that today Martinique in the Caribbean, Réunion in the Indian Ocean and Tahiti in the Pacific are more thoroughly part of the Fifth Republic than the Isle of Man or the Channel Islands are of the United Kingdom. Being featured in every weather forecast has not necessarily been great compensation for continued economic underdevelopment or, as in the case of French Polynesia, decades of nuclear testing within its territory.

Beyond these 'Overseas' regions, as they are called, France also pursued an aggressive strategy of maintaining economic dominance in its former African empire. Outside Algeria, France had, like Britain, disentangled itself from formal rule by assisting in the installation of relatively friendly liberation movements, and from the 1960s onwards built up a complex web of business and political connections known, more or less openly, as 'Françafrique'. The superficially dramatic French military intervention against Islamist terrorism in Mali in 2013 was part of a much longer project of continuing regional hegemony.[21]

The United States has of course remained a global superpower throughout these decades, but by the 1970s its own understanding of itself was becoming shaky. The 1973 oil crisis struck a nation dismayed by President Nixon's criminal attempts to cover up the Watergate scandal and resigned to a withdrawal from Vietnam, after 50,000 American combat deaths, that was very clearly a defeat for the USA. The presidency of Jimmy Carter from 1977 seemed to mark a further low point – Carter himself in a much-mocked speech portrayed the nation as beset with woes of its own making, a 'malaise' he could not remedy. The deaths in April 1980 of eight American troops in a botched attempt to rescue embassy personnel held hostage for over a year in revolutionary Iran drew a grim line under a legacy of failure that the new presidency of Ronald Reagan aimed self-consciously to eradicate.

Reagan now lives in American nationalist legend as the man who won the Cold War, and there can be no doubt that the vast and aggressive expansion of the American military he put in train (paid for, contrary to his professed economic principles, by escalating government debt from just over 25 per cent of GDP in 1980 to over 40 per cent by 1988) was part of the multidimensional crisis of internal political collapse that brought down the Soviet Bloc. Reagan's administration was nonetheless not immune to humiliating defeats. After a catastrophic suicide-bombing in Beirut in 1983 that killed 241 US Marines, sailors and soldiers, American forces withdrew from active engagement in Middle East peacekeeping for the remainder of the decade.

The hugely jingoistic posturing around relatively minor military operations – the ousting of a socialist government from the tiny Caribbean island of Grenada in 1983 (only days after the Beirut attack), the aerial bombing of Tripoli in revenge for a terrorist attack in 1986, the removal of Panama's President Noriega under Reagan's successor G. H. W. Bush in late 1989 – showed above all the cultural and political need for narratives of overt dominance.[22] Such narratives were, of course, complemented in reality by the darker struggle to maintain the USA's hegemony – the involvement of the CIA in the 1973 downfall of the Allende government in Chile being just one of many antidemocratic interventions justified by the overarching rhetoric of anti-communism. The 'School of the Americas' at Fort Benning, Georgia, taught counterinsurgency practices to military cadres from a swathe of right-wing dictatorships, many of whom went on to use violence, torture and selective assassination to control their populations, especially in the 'dirty wars' of the 1970s.[23] By the later 1980s, figures within the Reagan administration were prepared to break US law and secretly sell arms to their sworn enemy Iran, in order to divert the proceeds to Contra rebels in socialist Nicaragua, bypassing a congressional ban on funds for these forces. The justification put forward for this centred on securing Iranian goodwill towards the release of Western hostages held by militias in Lebanon – circling back to the humiliation of 1983.[24]

It is also important to remember that, however fondly Reagan's geopolitical triumphs are remembered, and how-ever much his military build-up stimulated some sectors of the economy, there was no halt in the 1980s to a steady decline in the prosperity of the average US worker. Patriotic rhetoric then, as now, provided only a thin veneer over the reality of what was already dubbed the Rustbelt. Bruce Springsteen's 1984 lyrics to 'Born in the USA', so often mistaken for a patriotic anthem, speak in fact of the grim realities of life in an increasingly post-industrial America. Across the following two decades, into and out of a series of wars, economic bubbles and crashes, the economic condition of most Americans (like most Britons and French) has continued to decline.

A persistent accompaniment to this has been the culti-vation of external enemies on whom to project fear and anger. In the twenty-first century, despite the vast disparities in the realistic scale of their threats, Islamist terrorism has provided a solid long-term replacement for the Soviet Union; but, during the hiatus between the two, other foes were easily conjured up. American culture from the late 1980s became deeply hostile to Japanese economic encroachment, as real relative decline mixed with resentment that the loser of the Second World War could possibly threaten the winner's dominance. Japan as a looming power, doing something fundamentally dishonest and violating the natural order of things, could be treated as a background reality or as a key plot-point.

The uniquely Japanese *zaibatsu* economic cartels appeared as lurking villains in many works of speculative fiction. Michael Crichton's 1992 novel *Rising Sun* (turned into a film the following year) hinged on the culturally alien and supremely manipulative Japanese as economic invaders, while Tom Clancy's martial techno-thriller *Debt of Honor* (1994) imagined a second Pearl Harbor attack on US Pacific installations (and a Boeing 747 used as a giant kamikaze to destroy the US Capitol). Ironically, by the time this was published, Japan had already entered its 'lost decade' as overenthusiastic expansion led to a property-bubble collapse, and the US was newly uplifted by its post-Gulf-War status as global policeman. Two decades later, the same fears have been transferred to China with what appears to be significantly more practical justification if equally little real cultural awareness or willingness to consider an Asian power as an equal. Tom Clancy was ahead of the game, envisioning in 2000's *The Bear and the Dragon* a Chinese government invading Siberia in pursuit of hegemony before succumbing to the inevitable, and satisfyingly devastating, US riposte.

The history of the UK, France and the USA since 1945 is marked indelibly by a sense of entitlement to greatness. Throughout the decades since the end of *les Trente Glorieuses*, an increasingly financialised capitalism has developed, sustaining the wealth of the upper echelons of Western societies while their welfare states, and capacity to generate mass high-quality employment, have steadily diminished. Once localised as 'Thatcherism' or 'Reaganomics', the default academic response to this has been to define this economic model as 'neoliberalism', a new ultra-exploitative phase of global capitalism. This is now effectively an article of faith for many on the left, and in many ways it is a perfectly credible observation. However, from the point of view of the average voter, neoliberalism might as well not exist.

Where the academic language of neoliberalism seeks to place us all within a single worldwide structure of rising inequality, and there is strong public support for acting against key elements of that inequality within each society, our cultures overall reject the claim that we are all part of a homogenous global problem. The politics of the present instead place the greatness that is the electorate's birthright in an unjustly stolen, explicitly national, and nationalist, past – and increasingly seek to scapegoat others as responsible for the theft. Donald Trump's election slogan 'Make America Great Again' booms it out with particular vigour, but the logic of the Brexit campaign's 'Take Back

Control' is exactly the same. Marine Le Pen's most recent slogan, '*On est chez nous*', says more than just 'We are at home', its menacing subtext being: 'This is OUR home (and not yours, immigrant)'.

All three of these nations' political cultures are currently beset by ideas that promise a closed national labour market, a wide outflow of trade and the undisputed sovereign power to maintain those things for the benefit of the core, white, population. At first glance, this may seem like simple nostalgia for the imperial dominance that Orwell criticised, but it is in fact a distorted and demented version of the past. Britain, France and the USA never existed as entities that were both closed-off and commanding. Waves of immigration of all kinds shaped their populations even at the height of imperial splendour, while the cost of maintaining that empire, and the resistance to it, was crippling – and indeed, on this side of the Atlantic, this was a strong reason for hastening towards 'Europe' as a more rational and attainable form of greatness. Generations of politicians steered their countries through tempests and rapids where, looking back, many now see only the calm waters of a safe harbour.

It is easy to come up with answers for why different groups find different elements of the Trump, Brexit or Le Pen agendas attractive. A simple diagnosis of 'racism' will go a long way in many cases. But these sentiments run more deeply into the question of national identity: what it is, how it is built and above all how it imagines national populations in time and what their stories are. Attempting to define distinctive national cultures often sinks into the realm of self-parody – hot dogs, baguettes and Marmite;

how to pronounce the word 'scone'; regional cheeses; which particular forms of bad comedy one prefers. George Orwell himself once wrote at length (and highly questionably) on the way to make a perfect cup of tea. Ironically it is rare for any attention to be given to real structural national peculiarities: the English adversarial judicial system compared to the French inquisitorial one; the remarkable range of different powers enjoyed by individual US states; why Martinique or Guiana is a more integrated part of France than Jersey and Guernsey are of the UK... To do that would imply that peculiarities can be dissected and debated, rather than just cherished. And arguably, as these national cultures have lost the vigour that came with various forms of empire, and have moved into a period of ageing, cherishing their own peculiarities has become a refuge from reality.

Cultures that put a premium on national identity tend to invest it, paradoxically, with both longevity and youth. The latter is sometimes expressed literally: in the 1830s nationalists began to call themselves things like 'Young Italy' and 'Young Ireland'. The trend continued into the early twentieth century with the 'Young Turks', as an assertion that nationhood was a thing of vigorous youth, looking to the future, with the empires and potentates it sought to replace moribund, effete and doomed. The idea of youthful vigour was often invested in wider notions of growth, dynamism and expansion – for example, that the French had both a superior culture and the capacity to spread it to the world in a *mission civilisatrice*; that Britons 'never shall be slaves' and would see their empire set its bounds 'wider still, and wider'; and that it was

Americans' 'Manifest Destiny' to conquer their continent. This protected the idea of a long-lived national culture from the obvious risk of longevity: senescence.

Our Western societies are now dominated demographically by older people in a fashion unprecedented in history. This creates tremendous and as-yet-unresolved challenges for healthcare and the balancing of working and non-working populations. These problems are piled upon those of climate change and global competition, which help to drive concern, alarm and despondency about the future. It is tempting to heap responsibility for nationalist distortions directly on to the old: Baby Boomers have notoriously been blamed for stealing Millennials' future, and their place on the housing ladder, since before the last economic crash. And it is notable that, for example, the slope of support for Brexit rises steeply with age. In France, however, the slope runs the other way: Marine Le Pen's anti-system xenophobia strikes a stronger chord with the dispossessed young, living through a decade of 25 per cent youth unemployment, than with the old who still remember Vichy. Our current real and potentially fatal cultural dementia cannot be dismissed as merely the product of accumulated individual senilities.

The demands of contemporary 'populist' movements make manifest a vision of the past that is the opposite of a coherent history. Little more than a disconnected series of images, it is the political equivalent of the long-retired man who wakes up one morning and tries to leave for work in his pyjamas, or the woman who mistakes her son for her dead husband. In the individual, this dementia is a symptom of looming fatal decline. We risk the same fate for our societies. The politicians of earlier generations did not try to turn the clock back to what had never been. Even Margaret Thatcher, condemning to death the nationalised heavy industries of postwar Britain, had an understanding (agree with it or not) of why old ways could not continue, and a vision of new opportunities for new economic sectors (not least through helping to drag into existence the European single market).

There is something unprecedented and profoundly alarming in the eager reach for the past that now frames our future. Unverified rumours swirl that British ministers may have seriously used the phrase 'Empire 2.0' about future global trading arrangements. Fringe political ideas about the merits of the 'Anglosphere' and a potential 'CANZUK' bloc, based on former colonies' imagined affections for an increasingly distant shared imperial history, have nudged their way towards the mainstream. From the other end of the political spectrum, the militant former leader of the now-defunct National Union of Mineworkers, Arthur Scargill, has been quoted in the press as believing that Brexit will be an opportunity to reopen redundant coal mines and cotton mills.[25]

We can, variously, laugh at, lament and despair over such delusions, and each week's news brings fresh evidence of the superficial chaos such ideas have injected into politics. But, as we review the contours and underlying assumptions of those events, we can also reflect further on what they are symptoms of – on how we have come to lose contact with history, and what might be done to make the case for saving ourselves, before it is, indeed, too late.

2
Current Follies

One of the difficulties of living in the present political moment is that you never know what is going to go wrong next. As I write, the Labour Party's Shadow International Trade Secretary has just been reported as saying that nothing short of a definitive Hard Brexit, cutting the UK off from all institutions of the EU, would be in the country's real interests – and indeed, that trying to remain connected with Europe opened the road to 'disaster' or to the UK becoming a 'vassal state' (which is apparently what Norway is now).[1] Meanwhile, the actual International Trade Secretary has found the time to write to the BBC accusing it of a 'clear pattern of unbalanced reporting of the EU economy', a month after the Leader of the Commons demanded that broadcasters be more 'patriotic' in their treatment of Brexit.[2] No doubt in a month's time there will be new appalling news, although quite possibly there will also still be absolutely no movement in practice towards figuring out what Brexit actually means.

As this peculiarly British set of problems continues to fester, Emmanuel Macron, elected President of France on either a tidal wave of enthusiasm or the backwash of the utter collapse of the Parti socialiste, according to taste, has just sacked his army chief of staff in another of a continuing series of ugly rows about what governance means in practice.[3] For 2017's Bastille Day celebrations, he welcomed Donald Trump to Paris for events that included a truly epic public handshaking contest, and which otherwise seemed designed to pamper the monstrous ego of the President of the United States. That president sits currently at the nexus of truly astonishing events. From here it is simply impossible to predict the next moves. Will Russia leak devastating evidence of electoral collusion? Will Trump sack the men appointed to investigate his family? Will he be impeached? Will he literally pardon himself? All of these things, imaginable only as a black farce a few short years ago, are now well within the bounds of possibility.[4]

Amid the daily flow of mind-boggling stupidity, it is necessary to take some steps back – first to recall the general shape of the situation that has overwhelmed conventional politics in the UK, USA and France in the last two years, and then to relate this to the larger shape of the historical context from which it all comes, and which continues to structure the ongoing folly of the present.

We can start with France, which of the three states seems to have evaded, at least for the moment, the collapse of its system towards the extremes. This has nonetheless happened through the real collapse of the established political parties, currently replaced in government by a new and wholly untried movement. Whatever 'Macronism' turns out to be, underlying and preceding it in recent years has been a sharp swing to the far right. The dominant factor in French politics since the popularity of President Hollande began to collapse in 2014 has been Marine Le Pen and the Front national. In dozens of polls since then, she led the presidential field, attracting 28–30 per cent of preferences, dipping only slightly in late 2016 as right-of-centre voters had a honeymoon with the candidacy of François Fillon and then sliding in the final weeks of campaigning down to her score of 21.3 per cent in the first round of actual voting in April 2017. This was nonetheless enough to put her through in second place against Macron's 24 per cent for the run-off vote. For this, polls put her vote-percentage in the mid to high forties in six of the twelve regions of France, and a swathe of national polls put her as high as 41 per cent of the overall vote in late April and early May. Her final score of 33.9 per cent effectively doubled what she had achieved for her party in the 2012 election.

While this election saw a sharp rise in abstention, to just over 25 per cent, it nonetheless saw a substantial proportion of voters prepared to cast their ballot for a party that carries the traditions of the French extreme right – traditions it is accurate to call fascistic despite, as we shall see later, the superficial 'de-demonisation' Le Pen has undertaken.[5] The subsequent two-round legislative elections appeared to push the FN back to the margins, eventually winning only eight seats, but in the first round they outscored both the Parti socialiste and its further-left rival La France insoumise, and were within touching distance of the conventional-right party Les Républicains. Although Macron's République En Marche swept to an apparent landslide it was in a second round of voting where a staggering 57.4 per cent of registered voters abstained, and a further 9.9 per cent spoiled their ballots.[6] Almost exactly two-thirds of the electorate rejected the whole system; and, as things stand, many of their resentments will be fertile ground for further Front national gains in future. The very speed and sweeping gains of Macron's new movement makes it fragile; and when even an organisation like the Parti socialiste, which has endured for more than a century, can collapse within five years to virtual irrelevance, only a great optimist would declare that no further ruptures are possible.

The USA appears to have undergone its own massive, system-breaking rupture in the past two years. After announcing in June 2015 that he would be running for president, Donald Trump consistently occupied one of the top two spots in polling, and by the time the various states' primary elections for the Republican nomination began in the spring of 2016, he was often holding leads of 30 per cent or more over his nearest rivals.[7] He ultimately won forty-one of the fifty-six local contests and a substantial majority of the final convention delegates. Trump's shameless character benefited from remarkable levels of media attention, and even the revelation of remarks about molesting women that would have ended the career of a more conventional candidate seemed only to increase his attraction to the Republican base.

Trump ran to the hard right, collecting the endorsement of David Duke, the USA's most high-profile (former)

Ku Klux Klan leader, from the very beginning of his campaign, and persistently refusing to distance himself from such racist supporters.[8] He also succeeded decisively in making the abandonment of the white working classes of the Midwest a key campaign issue, creating a basis for victory in the region alongside a relentless deluge of abuse of every aspect of Hillary Clinton's character and record. Thanks to the electoral-college system, Trump won the national election on the basis of local victories in Pennsylvania, Ohio, Indiana, Michigan and Wisconsin, tipping the balance of the contest to him despite winning almost three million fewer votes than Clinton. With both houses of the US Congress also falling under Republican control, Trump appeared to have created a revolution.

During the same two-year period the politics of the United Kingdom have been in permanent crisis. It is difficult to remember that in May 2015 Prime Minister David Cameron secured the first Tory majority since John Major in 1992, confounding the pollsters while Labour collapsed to 30.4 per cent of the national vote and lost forty Scottish seats. At the time this seemed like an earthquake, but it brought with it the Conservative-manifesto promise of a renegotiation of the UK's European Union membership. Cameron delivered this in February 2016, with a package that would have consolidated the UK's status as exceptionally distanced from many of the EU's core obligations while also remaining a full voting member and participant in all its benefits.[9] With remarkable insouciance, this was put forward to a referendum in June 2016 as a direct in/out question about the EU. In campaigning, almost all major political figures struggled to summon up any enthusiasm for the EU, or any realistic sense of the risks of leaving it. The emotional initiative of the campaign was seized by the UK Independence Party, and primarily by Nigel Farage, its only remotely media-savvy figure, alongside the cartoonish presence of Boris Johnson, who had apparently weighed the possibility of campaigning to remain before plumping for the more rebellious option.

The final vote, a week after the Labour MP Jo Cox had been brutally murdered by a neo-Nazi yelling 'Britain first!', saw a thin majority of 51.9 per cent vote to leave the EU. These 17.4 million votes amounted to 37.4 per cent of registered voters, taking part in a referendum that was specifically defined as non-binding (unlike for example the 2011 referendum on the Alternative Vote electoral system, which had binding outcomes written into the law that created it). The Tory and Labour parties, however, decided to behave instantly as if only full obedience to the people's desires were possible. Jeremy Corbyn, nine months into his role as Labour leader, publicly called for the departure mechanism from the EU, Article 50, to be triggered immediately – thus offering fuel to the widespread suspicion that Labour's official 'Remain' stance had been sabotaged from inside.

Meanwhile, the Tory Party imploded. David Cameron announced his resignation immediately. Brexit campaigners Boris Johnson and Michael Gove, having been pictured looking almost physically sick after the results, fell out over making leadership bids. Gove used his announcement, via emails to journalists, to pre-empt Johnson, who hours later used a live press conference to announce melodramatically that he would not be standing. With Gove's campaign subsequently sinking almost without trace, all this rein-forced the impression that they had not believed they were going to win and had no plan if they did. After further brief tergiversations the sitting Home Secretary Theresa May, on record as a Remainer but keeping a very low profile during the campaign, became leader and prime minister without a vote after all the other candidates withdrew.

Despite this, with the Labour Party plunging into a renewed leadership contest, and sinking below 30 per cent in the polls, May's new government appeared impregnable. Legal challenges to the proposed triggering of Article 50 compelled the prime minister into a parliamentary procedure she had hoped to avoid, but Labour's con-viction that the referendum result was unchallengeable ensured a smooth passage for the required Bill in March 2017. At the end of that month, after the EU had been formally notified, the Tories enjoyed a lead over Labour that nudged twenty points. Jeremy Corbyn's re-election by some 313,000 enthusiastic Labour supporters the previous September seemed to have condemned the party to irrelevance, bottoming out at 23 per cent in a YouGov poll on 13 April.

It was, no doubt, this above all else that tempted Theresa May to do what she had spent months swearing she would not do and call a snap general election, overriding the Fixed Term Parliaments Act with the collusion of all the main parties. The following seven weeks were witness to an astonishing spectacle as the Tory Party, campaigning on the content-free mantra of 'Strong and Stable Government', was forced to publicly reverse a flagship manifesto policy on meeting the costs of social care for the elderly, excoriated as a 'Dementia Tax', and the prime minister spent much of the campaign apparently hiding from voters at 'events' in empty warehouses. Meanwhile, Corbyn launched a barnstorming crusade on the basis of a lengthy manifesto for change (that nonetheless rigorously ruled out opposing Brexit), and rose relentlessly in the polls. With UKIP, who had regularly polled at 12 or even 14 per cent before the campaign, collapsing into near-invisibility without Nigel Farage at their head, pollsters had difficulty tracking all the variables in play, and only a minority identified that the Tory majority was actually at risk.

The final election results in the early hours of 9 June showed that everyone had lost. The Liberal Democrats gained a handful of seats, but saw their national vote-share slump even further; the SNP lost twenty-one of their fifty-six seats; UKIP's vote collapsed to less than a fifth of what it had been in 2015; Labour, despite gaining 40 per cent of the vote, an almost hallucinatory figure considering where they began, remained more than sixty seats short of where they would need to be to form a government. Prime Minister Theresa May faced the world having thrown away her party's slim but workable majority, and was forced in the following weeks into a deal with the Democratic Unionist Party's ten MPs for a wafer-thin majority – the DUP itself being so mired in scandal that power-sharing arrangements in Northern Ireland had collapsed around it before the campaign began.

In the late summer of 2017, Tories and Labour appeared to be in strengthening agreement – at least across their front benches – that the UK is committed to a Brexit that will be as 'hard' and definitive as possible. Indeed the only detectable disagreement about the mechanisms of Brexit is how long some kind of temporarily 'softened' transitional arrangement should last.[10] Tory convictions that there is a leading global role for a buccaneering, free-trading UK with whom everyone will be eager to make advantageous deals meet Labour certainties that freedom from the shackles of EU policy will allow the heirs of Tony Benn, the standard bearer of the hard Labour left in the 1980s and an ardent opponent of the European project, to finally build a socialist nation in splendid sovereign isolation.

Both sides are, in their different ways, mesmerised by visions that have no relationship to how Britain's economy and society have actually developed in the last generation. The gap between the political chaos that has reigned since the Brexit vote, and the blithe assurances of what the future holds, is staggering. Indeed, a whole array of informed political, economic, legal and social commentators continues to stagger under the awareness of looming folly, yelling into a void from which echoes back an incoherent noise, the dominant note of which sounds a lot like 'Immigrants!'[11]

In these conditions anything might happen before this book reaches publication. But these conditions are themselves symptomatic of wider and longer trends, and their short-term threats to civil society echo the deeper damage inflicted on the politics of the West. One of the terrible ironies already visible in the Brexit process has been the stunned outrage with which well-educated, middle-class white people who happen to be citizens of other EU countries have responded when threatened by the UK Home Office with the callous, off-hand treatment that is meted out to non-white people wrestling with nationality and immigration law every day. They and their supporters are right to be appalled at their own treatment; but, like almost everyone else, they have been quietly ignoring what happened to other kinds of people for a very long time.

The Council of Europe's Commissioner for Human Rights published in July 2017 a stinging rebuke to common attitudes on race, denouncing them as systematic 'Afrophobia'. Stretching from the vilification of politicians, and particularly female politicians, of African origin, to widespread and officially documented systematic police discrimination and brutality against non-white populations, Nils Muižnieks' judgment is harsh:

> The position of Black people in Europe needs to be strengthened, irrespective of whether it concerns recent migrants from Africa or already established Black communities. European states must first come to terms with their own past. To this end, those that have not done so should publicly acknowledge that slavery, the slave trade and colonialism are among the major sources of current discrimination against Black people.[12]

Countless screeds have been written about the kind of politics that Trump, Le Pen, Farage and their supporters represent. It has often been said that all of this can be lumped under the label of 'populism', and that it sits amid a basket of legitimate concerns that lower-income populations have about that other great academic catchall, neoliberalism.[13] Elaborate arguments have been had about just how far the expression of such concerns is indeed legitimate, in the context of the evils of neoliberalism, and how far the rise of populist leaders needs to be recognised as a genuinely popular response to the dangers posed to Western welfare states by unrestrained global capitalism. In these arguments, populism is often treated as if it should be seen as a worthwhile counterpoint to a heartless, distant technocracy, a recovery of the value of community and the right of the common people to be heard.[14]

This is mostly hogwash. Populist movements have a long and dishonourable history of peddling simple answers to complex questions of economic distress. Those simple answers are founded on the shared racial privilege of the target audience, and on the singling-out of other groups as the instruments of good people's undoing. From their modern origins in the late-nineteenth-century USA, into and out of the era of fascism, through the Cold War and decolonisation, down to contemporary opposition to the EU and the UN, populist movements lurch as if magnetically attracted towards conspiracy theories about global elites that always end up at a form of closeted or indeed overt antisemitism. On the way, they usually have profoundly nasty things to say about anything and anyone that comes between them and a backward-looking vision of homogenous, orderly communities. Emotional discomfort at change is used as a blanket condemnation of diversity in habits and expectations, and above all of differences in ethnicity, sexuality and culture. Whatever potentially legitimate concerns anyone might have, a populist response will turn them into a potent mixture of self-pity and detestation of difference.

Legitimising such responses also opens the dangerous road to accepting the brutal agendas of those who encourage and manipulate them. Steve Bannon, until August 2017 Donald Trump's 'chief strategist', proved himself a master at such manipulation, steering the right-wing website Breitbart News Network after the death of its founder. He has been widely reported as a student of various European thinkers of the fascist era, including the Frenchman Charles Maurras and the Italian Julius Evola.[15] He has also repeatedly made much of the idea that the contemporary world situation resembles that of *The Camp of the Saints*, a French novel of the early 1970s that makes a luridly and violently racist call for a white fightback against literal invasion from the non-white world. Shifting fluidly between a message of racial survival and the threat of Islamist terrorism, Bannon's use of the book's underlying idea of race war helps connect military and demographic 'threats' into one big, alarmist picture.[16]

Curiously, although translations of the book were known in right-wing circles in the USA, Bannon appears to have begun mentioning it publicly only after Marine Le Pen recommended it to her followers online in September 2015.[17] She has long claimed it as an inspiration, reportedly having read it for the first time at the age of eighteen. Although such connections were pushed below the radar as Le Pen concentrated on her de-demonised profile, she retorted sharply in January 2017 when an interviewer suggested that she was following Trump's success: 'I don't take Trump as a model; he's the one who's putting into effect what I have proposed for years and what our political opponents always said was absurd!'[18]

Commissioner Muižnieks' words take us to the heart of what is not being said when politicians follow 'the voice of the people' down these paths. The communities in a position to articulate populist sentiments are ones raised up by a history of racial privilege, and by the workings of that privilege as an integral component of social and economic inequality that remains searingly unjust on the global scale. Many great texts have already been written on the direct impact of these inequalities, and a very large book could be written simply to summarise the iniquities involved. What is presented here does not seek to do that, but rather to emphasise that such privilege and prejudice is the product of history, and that wider histories are bringing this situation to an end – or could be, if the political and cultural mainstream of Western nations were not gripped by a demented urge to deny that reality. What the USA, France and the UK undoubtedly share, at this crisis-wracked point in their history, is the complete failure as societies to meaningfully come to terms with their national pasts.

3

Shadows of Greatness

What has made us an Ingenious, Active and Warlike Nation... What has rendered us a Great, Wealthy, and Happy People... and what is it has made us Terrible to the whole World, but our English Liberty?[1]

I t is almost 300 years since this rambunctious rhetorical question was asked and answered in a combative political pamphlet of the 1720s. Allowing for occasional scruples at being seen as 'Terrible to the whole World', it seems nonetheless likely that its central message continued to resonate within the political mainstream for most of that time – and almost certain that, in the Age of Brexit and Trump, patriotic boosters on both sides of the Atlantic would still claim it as an admirable sentiment.

Whether framed by the narrative of 'Whig history' that gave us these notions of martial liberty – and American concepts of 'Manifest Destiny' – or by the parallel French conviction of being 'the Great Nation' with a 'civilising mission' to the world, Western notions of cultural and institutional superiority were born out of long histories of conflict. These propositions were used to whip up support for aggressive global action, playing assertions of strength against fears of weakness and claims of unity against the dread of subversion and defeat. The national bodies of America, France and Britain always felt themselves to be under attack, even as they exercised global power through technological, economic and military dominance.

The USA was born in fear of subversion, and of the idea that tyrannical power was plotting to turn 'merciless Indian savages' against the white population – those words made it into the final draft of the Declaration of Independence, while even more paranoid fears of slave insurrection were edited out. Before the end of the eighteenth century the new republic crafted a series of Alien and Sedition Acts authorising the detention and expulsion of dangerous foreigners. In the following generation, the Indian Removal Act of 1830 led to a genocidal process of ethnic cleansing in the lands east of the Mississippi. Scarcely had this great and tragic purge been completed than fears of immigration by 'un-American' Irish Catholics prompted the rise of the 'Know-Nothings' across the nation. These vehemently Protestant 'nativists' stormed the polls in the 1840s and early 1850s by drumming up the danger of subversion by racially inferior peoples loyal to the Pope. Their membership peaked at around a million before being undermined by scandals and the looming wider confrontation over slavery.

Fear of widespread slave uprising was endemic to slave-holding as a system, given new life at the end of the eighteenth century by the example of what became the Haitian Revolution. Contamination by the ideas and bodies of 'French negroes' sent waves of panic through the South. Slavery nurtured a fear of subversion as savage and all-embracing as the institution itself, with 'slave patrols' of white men routinely empowered to police the movements of the non-white population, up to and including the arbitrary execution of runaways.[2] In the 1860s, defence of this system was so ingrained that the resultant Civil War was ground out over four years of campaigning, causing around three-quarters of a million deaths – more than 2 per cent of the entire population. In the post-Civil War landscape of Reconstruction, violent resistance to black people being incorporated into society and politics helped give birth to the Ku Klux Klan, reasserting a romantic myth of Southern civilisation and doing it by intimidation and murder.[3] Robert O. Paxton, an eminent historian of fascism, has pointed to the KKK and its well-publicised methods as a forerunner and literal inspiration for later European movements.[4]

The history of the twentieth century merely recapitulates much of this earlier record of fearful hate – continued endemic racial discrimination, antisemitism, the extermination of socialist movements that were often led by immigrant communities, the scare over international communism prompting deportations from the time of the First World War onwards, the refounding of the Klan in the 1920s, blanket detention of 'untrustworthy' Japanese-Americans after Pearl Harbor, more 'Red scares' and

McCarthyism in the nuclear age, and so on down to the continually traumatised, racially divided society of today. One recent strand of academic history has even highlighted the extent to which US Jim Crow racial laws were the model for Nazi plans to incorporate open discrimination into the German legal system.[5] Public lynchings remained commonplace through the first half of the twentieth century. Most of some 700 monuments to Confederate causes in American cities were put up after 1910. A significant number were put up in the 1960s and 1970s.[6]

Britain and France, meanwhile, spent much of their modern history engaged in traumatising each other with the threat of internal subversion and moral dissolution. From the Restoration of Charles II in 1660 onwards, French royal support for Stuart tendencies towards Catholicism aroused the same paranoia that Spanish deeds had a century earlier. The Bill of Rights that framed the desires of the 1688 Glorious Revolution denounced James II for causing 'good Subjects being Protestants to be disarmed at the same time when Papists were both Armed and Imployed contrary to Law'. Many of those 'papists' were Irish; and several years' conflict in Ireland followed, adding to the alarm of encirclement. These fears were perpetuated by the 1715 and 1745 Jacobite Rebellions in Scotland, led by Stuart pretenders openly backed by France.

The imperial battle for North America and India that raged through the eighteenth century continued to carry on both sides a freight of anxiety about subversion and dissolution. As late as 1780 rumours of secret royal Catholic rites and Jesuit infiltrators fuelled the massive 'Gordon

Riots' in London, while French elites hostile to the cor-
rosive impact of the Enlightenment saw Freemasonry – a
new import from the Anglophone world that had become
fashionable in the salons of the Parisian elite and beyond
– as a wicked anti-Catholic plot.

The French Revolution of 1789, and the Terror that
followed, was, for such reactionaries, proof enough that
they had been right all along, while in Britain it prompted
new waves of alarm as a new set of 'French ideas' threatened
to overturn the monarchy and established social order
alike. For an entire generation, near-hysterical suppres-
sion of dissent accompanied the more familiar epic of
the Napoleonic Wars, culminating most memorably in the
Peterloo Massacre of 1819 – men, women and children
cut down by the sons of the propertied classes serving
as volunteer cavalry, enraged at the apparent threat a
peaceful march for political reform posed to the structure
of their nation.

Both Britain and France in the nineteenth century soared
far enough ahead of the rest of the world economically
and imperially that some of these fears went into abeyance
– though both wrestled with the alarming consequences of
industrialisation and the rise of socialism in their different
and sometimes brutally violent ways. Never actually at
war with each other after Waterloo, the two powers were
sufficiently uneasy to find themselves in an arms race in
the 1860s, less than a decade after allying against Russia
in the Crimea. Monumental fortifications on England's
south coast and around key naval bases, redundant before
they were even finished, were one result.

Both nations, like the USA, were shaped by waves of

immigration throughout the century and into the next, in an age when the economic migration of millions from poorer regions was accepted as a fact of life and the reputation of all three countries as refuges for those fleeing more overtly authoritarian and persecuting regimes was real – despite the laments of nativist prejudice. Karl Marx lived in Paris for several years in the 1840s, then in London for decades, famously working on his theories in the reading room of the British Museum, while also being a correspondent and columnist for the *New York Tribune*.

In their twentieth-century histories, both Britain and France faced the contradictions of being globe-spanning empires – based on increasingly elaborate notions of cultural, scientific, military, technological, economic and 'racial' superiority – and of seeing those empires end. In 1908 Evelyn Baring, recently retired British proconsul in Egypt, published his authoritative account of *Modern Egypt*, showing the heights to which such notions routinely reached. For Baring, the 'trained intelligence' of the European worked 'like a piece of mechanism', while 'The mind of the Oriental, on the other hand, like his picturesque streets, is eminently wanting in symmetry'.

Baring deployed his long experience as an administrator to generalise: notwithstanding any ancient achievements, Egyptians were now 'singularly deficient in the logical faculty. They are often incapable of drawing the most obvious conclusions from any simple premises of which they may admit the truth.' Under questioning, such a person 'will probably contradict himself half-a-dozen times before he has finished his story. He will often break down under the mildest process of cross-examination.'[7]

Generations of imperial civil servants and policemen who had sternly and disapprovingly filled out their reports as 'Orientals' quailed before them found themselves within the space of only one lifetime cast out of their positions, forced to watch the expanding bounds of empire shrink and attempts at assertion, like Suez in 1956, end in further humiliation.

As those generations have passed into the grave, they have been replaced by others whose experience of national glories is almost entirely second-hand. Nigel Farage, for example, may recently have solemnly declared that every patriot needed to see the film *Dunkirk*, but he was born in 1964, a year after *The Great Escape* first hit cinemas with its message of derring-do (based on reality but also, with its fabricated American leads, delivering a certain kind of fantasy in its place). Nigel was a small boy when *Battle of Britain* came out in 1969 – though he seems to have missed its acknowledgement of the valiant role of Polish airmen in the struggle. As documented by an acquaintance of his 1970s schooldays, he may perhaps already have been en route to a preference for Nazi marching songs – something he could have picked up from *Battle of the Bulge*, first released when he was still a toddler.[8] The repeated assertion by middle-aged men of the patriotic duty that events twenty or thirty years before they were born impose on the whole nation would be amusing were it not also a grim reminder of how deeply ingrained a whitewashed and heroic construction of the imperial past remains.

While some make bold assertions about what the glorious past demands we do, it remains trivially easy to show how the long history of imperial dominance continues to cast a shadow – or indeed a stain – over public life. In November 2016, the UK government confirmed that more than 1,500 Chagos islanders, forcibly removed from their homes in the Indian Ocean half a century ago to make way for a massive airbase, were definitively barred from returning. Admitting that the 'manner' of the original removal had been 'wrong' and was now a matter of 'deep regret', the Foreign Office nonetheless said 'defence and security interests, and cost to the British taxpayer' prevented resettlement of the islands. A commitment of £40 million 'over the next decade' was intended to soften the blow – though of course only decades of campaigning and litigation by the islanders and their supporters had produced any response at all.[9]

Meanwhile, in a far larger and grimmer matter, the UK government continues to contest the claims of tens of thousands of people allegedly tortured by British authorities during the 1950s Mau Mau Rebellion in Kenya. Having been forced to settle initial claims – and to admit to the existence of massive quantities of previously hidden administrative records – the UK now seeks to deny further liability.[10] One of its most recent manoeuvres, in the spring of 2017, was to claim in court that some testimony about misleading ministerial statements in the 1950s might be punishable as 'contempt of parliament'.[11]

The persistent relics of empire are literally global. With the single exception of New Zealand's administration of the tiny island territory of Tokelau, every single 'non-self-governing' territory listed by the United Nations with an 'administering power' is controlled by the UK, USA, or France.[12] Guam and its neighbouring Northern

Marianas Islands, American Samoa, and the US Virgin Islands, along with Puerto Rico (which is not on that list), are home to American citizens who, because of their territories' quasi-colonial status, do not enjoy the same political representation as those of the fifty states. As long ago as 1993, 'globalisation' was already exploiting this situation. Saipan in the Marianas was the home of ruthless sweatshops staffed by migrant labourers whose products carried lucrative 'Made in USA' labels.[13] Similar scandals about American Samoa erupted a decade later.[14] Criminal prosecutions dealt with the worst cases of working conditions little better than slavery but the dependence of these territories on cheap labour continues, as does their anomalous status that encourages such practices.[15]

In France's assorted overseas departments and territories, relative poverty and neglect continue to be serious problems. Per capita GDP of the French Caribbean departments, Martinique and Guadeloupe, is barely half that of Metropolitan France; that of French Guiana, despite the presence of the European space programme, lower still. The Pacific territory of New Caledonia enjoys a per capita GDP higher than the metropole, but much of this is generated by exports of nickel whose benefits do not reach the general population. Persistent separatist unrest abated nearly twenty years ago with agreement on routes towards a future independence referendum, now looming in 2018.[16] With continuing discontent at high levels of unemployment, social dislocation and violence, President Macron has nonetheless spoken out against a 'rupture to the common history shared with France' when the vote occurs.[17] Just north of New Caledonia, incidentally, is

57

Vanuatu, which until 1980 was ruled as the New Hebrides in a truly bizarre colonial 'condominium' by rigorously equal teams of British and French administrators.

French concern to maintain itself as a literally global power transcends political divisions. Since the end of the Second World War, France has maintained economic influence in Western and Central Africa through the CFA-Franc currency. CFA once stood for Colonies françaises d'Afrique but now instead means Communauté Financière Africaine; it serves fourteen states through two regional central banks and is intimately tied to France, where much of the cash reserves of the system are held. It may not be true that, as some sensationalist internet headlines repeat, these nations are 'Forced by France to Pay Taxes for the "Benefits" of Colonialism', but it is hard to deny that the fundamental links forged before independence persist.[18]

Throughout the later decades of the twentieth century, and into the twenty-first, a network of corrupt economic and political connections bound French businesses and politicians to a series of dictatorial rulers who flourished under their former colonial masters' protection. This system was widely known as 'Françafrique' but also punned brutally as 'France à fric', likening it to a cash-dispenser for political bribery and slush-funds.[19] Oil revenues from Gabon were a central part of the arrangement, and the source of much of the cash that swilled back and forth between Paris offices and presidential palaces. Leaked documents in 2009 linked the election campaigns of both Jacques Chirac and Nicolas Sarkozy to huge amounts embezzled in Gabon from one of the CFA-Franc's central banks. President Hollande throughout his time in office promised to end this net of relationships, but there is no evidence of France relinquishing its basic role as overseer of the region and its political machinations.[20]

Britain cannot look on the French role in Africa with any smugness. It controls a majority of territories the UN lists as 'non-self-governing', and three of those – Bermuda, the British Virgin Islands and the Cayman Islands – come close to the top of any list of notorious global tax havens (along with Jersey and the Isle of Man, peculiar historic jurisdictions within the European sphere). Only in 2013 did these territories agree to enter into a slightly more transparent set of arrangements, yet in 2016 the UK government was still refusing to press them to relax the secretive company-ownership laws that are a chief component of their tax-haven status.[21] UK authorities hide behind the quasi-independence of these states to avoid responsibility for the widespread illegality of the kind revealed in the 'Panama Papers' investigation.[22]

The UK's historical role as an empire still sits at the centre of what was once the British Commonwealth and is now the Commonwealth of Nations. As an organisation, this has floated for decades between an explicit founding intention to maintain empire-like connections on a more equal basis – but with Britain implicitly central – and a more decentred ambition to promote values that, like 'British values' in domestic discussion, are supposedly distinctive but are indistinguishable in practice from universal human rights. Maintaining the respectable veneer of membership has often seemed to take precedence over any concern with such rights, leading to rows as recently as 2011 over the cynical adoption of lip-service declarations by member states.[23] A new Charter of the Commonwealth signed in 2013 embraced a wide range of opposition to discrimination, but conspicuously failed to put in place any mechanisms for action over, for example, the many members still operating laws against homosexuality. If the Commonwealth is not the neo-colonial cash-machine that Françafrique represents, it might justly be called a comfort blanket of prestigious but unenforced good intentions.

The idea of the Commonwealth has intruded into the Brexit debate in ways that reveal more about the sometimes-fatuous sense of privilege surrounding UK politics. In January 2015, a group calling itself the Commonwealth Freedom of Movement Organisation was founded. This was not, as one might have hoped, a lobby for a less restrictive – and less racial – approach to such movement between richer and poorer nations. The CFMO, which relaunched as CANZUK International two years later, presented itself as 'the world's leading non-profit organisation advocating freedom of movement, free trade and foreign policy coordination between Canada, Australia, New Zealand and the United Kingdom'.[24] Its website displays eight men, seven of whom are conspicuously white, as 'our team', including Andrew Lilico, a former Conservative economic adviser and notable public advocate for Brexit.

Lilico's perspective on history and identity can be gauged from a recent exchange on social media, where, in the course of a few tweets, he moved from arguing that widespread British pride in the history of empire was an undeniable fact of contemporary life to proposing as self-evident that 'The British Empire was vastly more humane, liberal, self-sacrificing, self-restrained & morally driven than its competitor states.'[25] Lilico is also one of the fourteen individuals – all white men – shown on the parallel website of CANZUK Uniting, which bills itself as 'your source for comment and analysis, promoting political and economic unification among the peoples of Canada, Australia, New Zealand and the United Kingdom'.[26] Intriguingly, on this site, six of the fourteen white men appear to be based in – and are perhaps citizens of – the USA.[27]

One of the others is Andrew Roberts, the splenetically right-wing historian who in 2006 published *A History of the English-Speaking Peoples Since 1900*, updating Winston Churchill's famous work and jingoistically boosting the Anglosphere as the best of everything on the planet.[28] In September 2016, Roberts pontificated that Brexit provided 'many splendid opportunities', of which 'perhaps the greatest is the resuscitation of the idea of a CANZUK Union'. In this piece, as in others by Lilico, much ingenuity is exercised to claim that current arrangements (the EU, but also for example NAFTA) are obsolete and defunct, and to suggest that historical cultural similarity, the existence of cyberspace, and visa-free personal mobility are key ingredients for allowing a 'union' of four states that literally span the globe to 'retake her place as the third pillar of Western Civilization' – alongside the conspicuously more compact USA and a 'United States of Europe'.[29]

Although a handful of conservative politicians outside the UK have gestured towards the thought that some elements of this might be a nice idea, none has pushed it anything like this far.[30] In Roberts' vision, arranging the future is an almost childishly simple matter of recolouring some maps to restore a sensation of emotional harmony and loyalty. John Elledge in the *New Statesman* has pointed out how other Brexit and CANZUK advocates enjoyed childhoods in exotic corners of the world that were more like those of the imperial ruling class than of most modern Britons.[31] To them an Anglosphere makes emotional sense, while freedom of movement across the Channel does not. But there is a strong sense in which the whole CANZUK concept concentrates the cultural dementia of this moment into a particularly intense form.

Purely economically, it is almost meaningless – Canada and the UK both send no more than 3 per cent of their exports to the other three CANZUK partners. Australia's 5 per cent and New Zealand's 22 per cent on the same basis reflect trade between them as actual neighbours. New Zealand's exports to the UK make up only 3.4 per cent of its total, whereas 18 per cent of its products go to China; 56 per cent of all Australian exports go to China, Japan and South Korea. Meanwhile 77 per cent of Canadian exports go to its massive southern neighbour. Even the UK currently exports nearly three times as much to the EFTA countries (Iceland, Liechtenstein, Norway and Switzerland) as it does to CANZUK states; added to the 44 per cent it sends to the EU, this makes a clear majority of all its overseas trade. CANZUK as a replacement for EU membership is an idea any rational political actor should be embarrassed to put forward.[32] When it is proposed as some kind of cultural reunification of Western civilisation, that embarrassment should calcify into shame.

To consider it as a question of demography, there are for example almost as many people of South Asian origin in the UK (3.08 million, or 4.9 per cent of the population in 2011) as there are people of European origin in New Zealand (around 3.24 million, 69 per cent of 4.23 million in 2013). A quarter of the New Zealand population are Maori or Pacific Islanders, and most of the rest originate from Asia. Of Canada's 35 million population, some 5 million people – 15 per cent – identify as ethnically French, almost as many as Irish and almost 10 per cent as German. Italians and Chinese both number more than 1 million. Almost 4 per cent are of South Asian origin. Hundreds of thousands more come from almost every European country; 4.2 per cent of Canadians (1.37 million) identify as First Nations and a further 1.36 per cent (447,000) as Métis, a distinct ethnicity with its origins in historical French intermarriage with First Nations peoples.

Of Australia's some 25 million population, some 11 per cent identify as ethnically Irish, 5.6 per cent Chinese, just under 5 per cent either Italian or German, almost 3 per cent Indian, almost 2 per cent Greek and 1.6 per cent Dutch. Of the entire population in the 2016 census, 26 per cent were born overseas; and while that included 907,000 born in England, it also included 236,000 from the Philippines, 219,000 from Vietnam, 78,000 from Lebanon, 67,000 from Iraq and 54,000 from Nepal, among many others. The Indigenous population of Aboriginal peoples and Torres Straits Islanders numbers some 649,000, 2.8 per cent of the total.[33]

If any of these societies were ethnically homogenous, united around an Anglophone identity by anything more than linguistic convenience, then one might see a shred of sense in a CANZUK Brexit. But they are not. The United Kingdom is home to almost eight million people born in every other corner of the globe, together making up around one-eighth of the whole population.[34] When CANZUK advocates talk about free movement, who can we imagine that they mean? Do they really mean the polyglot, multi-ethnic inhabitants of already-global societies, or do they mean the imagined white Anglophone inhabitants of what were once Dominions under the empire?

These societies – good, open, democratic societies as they mostly are – are growing less Anglospheric by the day, and certainly less attuned to the common heritage Brexiteers proclaim. White settlement on lands belonging to First Nations, Maori or Aboriginal peoples, and all the mistreatment that followed, is no longer swept under the carpet of progress but is apologised for, however inadequately as yet.[35] Economically, Canada, Australia and New Zealand all have much more to gain by reinforcing links to Asia, and to Europe collectively, than by trying to build a bloc that would implicitly – dementedly – seek to rival them, and whose founding moment was marked by shamefully unabashed racist hostility to all foreigners.

National identities that were never actually fixed – being always tied to the power of a state to expand its boundaries, to absorb new populations or send off new colonists and administrators to the four corners of the globe – have spent the last few decades shrinking inwards, to the point where any mixing has begun to seem an existential threat. The real threat, however, lies in the attempt to reproduce a false image of a national community, built on an almost entirely mistaken understanding of the difference between present conditions and those that prevailed when such nationalist mythology was created.

To take an iconic example, Britain and France, as late as the 1960s, had the technological and financial clout to deliver the world's only operational supersonic airliner, and the economic hubris to believe it would pioneer routine supersonic travel for the whole world. What they created, in Concorde, was a marvellous piece of technology, and a beautiful thing. But even as it was brought into service, vastly over-budget and more than a decade after the 1962 treaty that cemented the collaboration, it was falling into the past. Partly thanks to the oil shock, a wave of optimistic international orders from almost twenty airlines were cancelled by 1975. Concorde struggled from the outset to be economically viable, and steadily declined into a white elephant, spending its last years largely on charter flights, famous only for being itself. The rest of the world remained unmoved.

To take an example from the other end of the spectrum of mundanity: many millions of British people today live in a variety of robust houses – Victorian villas, Edwardian terraces, spreading inter-war suburbs – that were laid out during the time of empire; as millions of the French inhabit both grand urban apartment-blocks and sprawling suburbs. The same power that oversaw the new roads and pavements, the water supply, drainage, sewerage, gas lines and eventually electrification of all those homes, ruled at the exact same time millions upon millions around the world who lived in absolute squalor – and did absolutely nothing to improve their lot. The poverty of the imperial periphery was productive of the wealth closer to its centre.

To walk the streets of an elegant French city or a neat British suburb today is to tread on the accumulated advantage of empire. In some ways, anything that can be pointed to as a product of history, in Britain, France or the slowly conquered land-empire of the USA, is by that very fact also a product of empire, so intimately connected have the long histories of expansion, exploitation and migration been. Of course, if you believe in ideas of national distinctiveness, your only thought about all this may be 'Good for us!' But even without dismissing such views as simply racist, we can see that they are also futile and self-defeating.

The capacity to accumulate all that privilege was an artefact of unique historical circumstances, in which a bewildering variety of technological and institutional innovations, from square-rigged sailing-ships to crop rotation, slave plantations to steam engines, maritime insurance to joint-stock companies, produced a historical social form uniquely suited to achieving a leading role in the world, and sustaining it – for several centuries – by any and all means necessary, including global industrialised war. But that age is over. Empire really did become unsustainably expensive, even as its combined pretensions to both dominance and progress tore at its conceptual heart. However states organise themselves internally now, whatever attention, lip-service, or scorn they give to democratic norms and ideals, the rest of the world is no longer lying supine at the feet of the West. Nothing will ever restore the epochal advantage that sustained such inequality, and the real danger is approaching that situation with fear and rage.

4
Toxic Legacies

Acres of print have been devoted to the various fears and resentments that have driven Trump, Brexit and the Front national.[1] While some voices on the left have been determined to interpret the experiences of older, poorer, white voters as a class-based anti-system revolt, others have insisted that it is folly to ignore the racism that underpins their alarms.[2] Overt accusations of racism have a complex toxicity – even Nigel Farage has angrily insisted that 'Nothing I have said is racist' – because they tend to land in a blind spot between a popular conception that racism is only ever direct personal hatred and the well-established fact that racism of other, more structural kinds permeates modern societies.[3] When the general secretary of the Fabian Society, the oldest think-tank of the UK Labour Party, can say that a left-wing agenda could be carried successfully to power, but 'you've got to sound patriotic' and appeal to those voters who are 'socially traditional', many other shibboleths of identity are being invoked.[4]

Yet we will remain paralysed by these kinds of language, if the wider realities they deny are not more fully recognised. The common sense of 'patriotic' identity – which is often in practice much closer to a nationalistic pride – embroils people in assumptions that have visible harmful consequences for anyone outside the core of that identity, and where the collective trajectory is towards further exploitation of a historical privilege that is, as much as it is anything else, racial. Overt personal racism is only one version of a deeper historical construction of identity-as-superiority, founded on a basis of exploitation that a vocabulary of social values and patriotism always functioned to both obscure and justify.

A microcosm of this was visible in the UK when activists at Oxford University campaigned in 2015 for the removal of a statue of Cecil Rhodes from Oriel College.[5] In an alternate universe, one might have had a long and interesting discussion about whether or not the four-foot-high image, rather awkwardly inserted into the neoclassical façade of a building funded by Rhodes' bequest, really did perpetuate imperialism in the same way a much larger and more prominent image of him in Cape Town, South Africa did until its removal earlier the same year.[6] However, in this universe, a deluge of scolding and hectoring was poured on the black students who voiced the demand.

Charles Moore in the *Telegraph* predictably lectured them on the folly of wasting their time protesting when they could have been thinking about the value of historical continuity.[7] John Simpson in the *New Statesman* was slightly more sympathetic in theory, while pointing out that bringing down a statue could not 'change the past' and gently patronising the disjuncture between genteel Oxford and the problems of South Africa one of the protest leaders had left behind to study at the university.[8] Professor Mary Beard, a notable voice for progressive opinions on other issues, made it clear both online and when quoted in the tabloid press that the protest was silly; the students were trying to have it both ways, to 'whitewash Rhodes out of history, but go on using his cash', and risked starting a 'great statue cull' that would be a self-evident folly.[9] A *Guardian* editorial wrung its hands over the fact that the protesters clearly were in the right on the larger issues, but wound up observing that 'to purge every trace of the past as though it never existed' was 'the fanatic's way' with 'disturbing echoes'.[10]

Within Oxford, a survey of the university's students found that 37 per cent wanted the statue removed, but public reaction continued to treat the issue as one of a small group of misguided zealots.[11] In December 2015 Oriel College agreed to an extended period of reflection and consultation about the statue's possible removal, but this was cut short at the end of January 2016 with a decision that the statue would stay. As reported in the press, a letter from the college's own fundraising chief a week earlier had noted a flood of correspondence overwhelmingly hostile to the potential removal and frequently threatening the withdrawal of financial support if it went ahead. It recorded 'a real sense of shame and embarrassment over what the College has done' in potentially bowing to protest, and 'most damaging' criticisms from 'distinguished academics', contributing to the potential loss of tens or even hundreds of millions in future donations.[12]

This small protest had clearly tapped into a significant vein of resentment at the idea of altering the fabric of the Oxford landscape for unacceptable reasons. Along the way, it brought out a series of arguments that connect up into a serious worldview: that the material fabric of the past is part of a 'history' that must be preserved; that at the same time too much should not be read into any particular part of it; but that as a whole it should always be treated gently, or indeed reverently. Coming from the nation whose troops, among many other things, looted and destroyed the vast splendours of the Summer Palace at Beijing not once but twice in the nineteenth century, and whose aircraft bombed Dresden into rubble in the twentieth, this is all rather rich.

The notion in particular that statues are just not important enough to make a fuss over stands in contrast to the recent polemics surrounding, for example, new statues of Mary Seacole (does it defame the memory of Florence Nightingale?),[13] Millicent Fawcett (just not really feminist enough?),[14] and Margaret Thatcher (so many reasons).[15] Groups around the country campaign unceasingly for statuary of their favourite historical figures, precisely because having such a monument is seen as *particularly* significant. And others campaign against them for the same reason. Statuary is highly political, and always has been – since the Israelites were forbidden to worship graven images; since the Protestant Reformation revived the injunction with a holocaust of iconoclasm (destroying the vast majority of late-medieval English public art); since the thousands of public monuments to the heroes of Marxism-Leninism were hauled down and smashed up (and turned into kitsch souvenirs) across Eastern Europe after 1989.

The extent to which British populations generally wish to see the history of imperialism as something that has been essentially disarmed by the passage of time is visible more broadly in the idea of renaming streets and landmarks. There are unsurprisingly few places in the former Soviet Bloc still named after Stalin, Lenin and their comrades, but remarkably many in the UK named after slave traders. The sentiment that local continuity outweighs the real significance of what such names represent is widespread: two-thirds of Bristol respondents, for example, objected in a newspaper poll to renaming the Colston Hall music venue, with 'airbrushing history' being predictably invoked against such change.[16] But, as one campaigner pointed out, the real airbrushing lies in pretending that the hall did not get its name from one of the many local sites honouring a leading participant in the Atlantic slave trade.

Edward Colston spent his later years working very hard to whitewash his own role in history by spreading his philanthropy so widely across Bristol that an annual remembrance service for him is still held in the city, almost 300 years after his death.[17] In the same city, the university's landmark Wills Memorial Building was constructed a century ago to honour the engagement of the Wills family – tobacco merchants since the 1780s, their fortunes solidly founded on slavery – with local philanthropy and education. A petition to rename it has gained little traction.

In Britain's other great slave-trade ports, the same issues

persist. Glasgow's Buchanan Street, the second-biggest shopping street in the UK after London's Oxford Street, is named, as are many other prominent urban features, for one of the city's eighteenth-century 'Tobacco Lords', whose wealth poured into the region from Virginia slave plantations. A move to temporarily and symbolically rename them in February 2017, proposed by a local Green Party councillor, fell flat. In Liverpool, the notion of tackling the substantial presence of slave traders in the city's geography was ruled out a decade ago, partly at least because of the risk to Penny Lane's tourist traffic – the name commemorates James Penny, a local shipowner and vehement defender of the slave trade.[18]

This problem is not unique to Britain. The French city of Nantes, utterly dependent on the slave trade for its wealth in the eighteenth and early nineteenth centuries, now hosts a significant open-air memorial installation on its quayside, invoking the realities of slavery and celebrating its abolition. But the history recorded on the website of the memorial itself is one of rejection and struggle: from 1985, when the local council refused to fund proposed research into this local history, to 1992, when a temporary exhibition was grudgingly permitted (and its proposed further display in Bordeaux rejected),[19] to 1998, when a commemorative sculpture on the quay was vandalised within days of being installed.[20] It took fourteen years from a decision that year to the final opening of the current memorial.[21]

Meanwhile, 2017 was the bicentennial of the naming of the monumental and picturesque central rue Kervégan after Christophe-Clair Danyel de Kervégan, who before entering local politics in the 1790s had a decades-long career as shipowner, merchant and slave trader. Other streets in the city named after slave traders include rue Guillaume-Grou, avenue Guillon, chemin Bernier and, according to some campaigners, up to a dozen others.[22] Similar numbers can be found in other ports such as La Rochelle and Le Havre and there is a particular concentration in Bordeaux, which, despite its modern preference for highlighting the history of wine, was heavily involved in the slave trade and beautified on its profits. Local campaigners have been seeking support for a memorial museum in the city for more than a decade, with so far little more than token success.[23] It is worth noting, by contrast, that the memory of Marshal Philippe Pétain, glorified all over France for his heroic leadership in the First World War, has been systematically erased from the streetscapes of the country, since his role as the puppet leader of the Vichy government.[24]

We must look to the USA to see how high the stakes of the game played out over the memorial landscape can be raised. In late April and early May 2017, the municipal government of New Orleans, Louisiana, finally succeeded, after many legal challenges, in removing four statues from sites in the city. Three of them represented Confederate leaders from the Civil War era, Robert E. Lee, Jefferson Davis and P. G. T. Beauregard, and the fourth commemorated a white-supremacist rising of 1874 against the multiracial administration of the city during the brief era of Reconstruction after that war. This monument was the first to be removed, under cover of darkness, by city workers who wore bulletproof vests, with balaclavas to conceal their identities, and drove trucks with their number-plates covered.[25]

The fear of armed resistance (which thankfully did not materialise) indicated the central place of ideologies of white supremacy in the historical landscape of the USA, where monuments of this kind, erected decades after the Civil War, continued to proclaim the virtues of that ideology unchallenged until the Civil Rights era, and where the 'Lost Cause' mythology of Southern moral rectitude lauded violent resistance to national government as a heroic component of national identity. A scathing piece by CNN journalist Steven Holmes pointed out that General James Longstreet, one of the South's most conspicuously effective leaders in the Civil War, is absent from this memorial landscape – because after that war he settled in New Orleans, rejected racism and led the 'predominantly black' militia forces that put down the 1874 rising.[26]

The Mayor of New Orleans, Mitch Landrieu, addressed these contexts publicly hours before the last of the four monuments was removed:

> These statues are not just stone and metal. They are not just innocent remembrances of a benign history. These monuments purposefully celebrate a fictional, sanitised Confederacy; ignoring the death, ignoring the enslavement, and the terror that it actually stood for. After the Civil War, these statues were a part of that terrorism as much as a burning cross on someone's lawn; they were erected purposefully to send a strong message to all who walked in their shadows about who was still in charge in this city.[27]

Landrieu went on to discuss the impact of ignoring the real history of enslavement and its consequences in compelling fashion, but he also positioned the ideology of the 'Lost Cause' as 'a false narrative of our history that I think weakens us' and looked towards an effort to 'make straight a wrong turn we made many years ago so we can more closely connect with integrity to the founding principles of our nation'.

As he moved towards the close of a speech which had opened with a roll-call of the many and varied peoples that had, willingly or unwillingly, contributed to the city's history, Landrieu invoked, un-ironically and indeed passionately, a vision of singular national unity:

> we now have a chance to create not only new symbols, but to do it together, as one people. In our blessed land we all come to the table of democracy as equals. We have to reaffirm our commitment to a future where each citizen is guaranteed the uniquely American gifts of life, liberty and the pursuit of happiness. That is what really makes America great and today it is more important than ever to hold fast to these values and together say a self-evident truth that out of many we are one.

It would be hard to find a more compelling illustration of the problem of historical consciousness in the USA than the juxtaposition between these words and the protection deemed necessary for those city workers going about removing a divisive monument. A notion of American national identity based on uncontroversially desirable 'founding principles', in which a message of equality in diversity can be grounded, is factually even less accurate than the Confederate legend of the Lost Cause, regardless of how desirable it might be to believe it.

A few weeks before these events, the *New York Times* columnist David Brooks had opined that the USA had 'lost' its story, 'the narrative that unites us around a common multigenerational project, that gives an overarching sense of meaning and purpose to our history'. That he could immediately assert that for 'most of the past 400 years' such an overarching story had existed in the 'Exodus story' that began with the 'Puritans', and squeeze in unreflectively the experience of black slaves – as if the USA for them was not in fact the bondage the Israelites fled from – illustrates the relentless power that an idea of national history has to overwhelm logic. Lamenting that 'Today's students get steeped in American tales of genocide, slavery, oppression and segregation', Brooks warned that 'American history is taught less as a progressively realised grand narrative and more as a series of power conflicts between oppressor and oppressed' and that the result of this was a swing to the right, as voters preferred 'religious nationalists' who could give them a sense of righteous purpose.[28]

Brooks as a writer is rarely other than platitudinous, but he is a high-profile commentator despite (or perhaps because of) this, and his lament was little less than a call to abandon critical thought for comforting mythology. A few months later, in August 2017, in Charlottesville, Virginia, an overtly neo-Nazi rally to 'defend' a statue of the Confederate General Robert E. Lee led to the death of a counter-protester, mown down by a car driven into the crowd by a known 'alt-right' partisan.[29] One ironic consequence of this horror was a sharp acceleration in the removal of Confederate monuments by local authorities, recognising their divisive viciousness.[30] A small shaft of light, in what is otherwise a darkening scene of rising extreme right-wing agitation, darkening still further each time President Trump has refused to distance himself from it.

Some, including noted academic experts, have said that it is a mistake to call the contemporary far right 'fascist': both because it lacks some of the overtly paramilitary and antidemocratic elements of previous movements and because the label itself is a historical one – like 'Bolshevik' – which loses meaning as it drifts from its original context.[31] One could ask in response why we still call things left- or right-wing, a label derived from the seating plan of the French National Assembly in 1789. But in the French case in particular, as the noted historian Jennifer Sessions has pointed out, the heritage of the Front national leads directly back to the fascism of the 1940s, by way of memories of colonial conflict and opposition to decolonisation.

The party's founder, Jean-Marie Le Pen, had volunteered to join the grim and ruthless war in Algeria in the 1950s, founded his first political organisations dedicated to preserving the empire, and in 1965 served as campaign manager for the presidential bid of Jean-Louis Tixier-Vignancour, an unrepentant survivor from the Vichy regime, in which he had served as head of censorship. As a lawyer, Tixier-Vignancour had defended only a few years earlier the leaders of the Organisation armée secrète (OAS), which had launched its own terrorist campaign against De Gaulle's 'surrender' of Algeria, trying to kill him several times. Vichy and Algeria were the twin causes that united many, if not most, of the supporters of the FN from its formal foundation in 1972.[32] As late as 1997, Jean-Jacques Susini, a notorious leader of the OAS once condemned to death for plotting De Gaulle's assassination, was welcomed as an FN candidate in Marseille. Jean-Marie Le Pen tweeted fond condolences on the death of this 'comrade' in 2017.[33]

The elder Le Pen, right down to his 'retirement' in 2011, maintained a basic attitude of chauvinism and aggressive white supremacy that peppered party programmes. Perennial policy goals included 'mass repatriation of non-European migrants, exclusionary reforms of French nationality law, and restrictions on immigrants' access to social security benefits'. Famously once charged for calling the Holocaust a 'detail of history', Le Pen could also barely contain his antisemitism – one reason why his daughter Marine, set on de-demonising the party, eventually ousted him unsentimentally from his own creation.

But by then, following his successful progression to the deciding round of the 2002 presidential election, securing 5.5 million votes, Le Pen's anti-immigrant agenda had begun to swing the whole right side of politics in its direction. Nicolas Sarkozy twice proposed immigration quotas based on 'regions of origin' – seeking to evade constitutional bans on ethnic or religious profiling – and in recent campaigning François Fillon proposed quotas based on a nebulous capacity for 'integration'.[34]

Against this background, Marine Le Pen's recasting of the FN as a guardian of the French republican-secularist tradition against creeping 'Islamisation' has been shrewd politics. Its salience was demonstrated in the summer of 2016, when women were banned from wearing the so-called 'burkini' on beaches across southern France. Local mayors who introduced the bans covered a spectrum from the FN to the Parti socialiste, and many pledged to keep them in force despite a ruling from France's highest legal authorities that this action was a 'serious and manifestly illegal violation of fundamental freedoms'.[35] Even the socialist prime minister at the time, Manuel Valls, denounced the clothing as 'not compatible with the values of the French Republic'. Seemingly equating swimwear with the bloody and horrifying attack on 14 July holidaymakers in Nice the month before, Valls affirmed that 'In the face of provocation, the nation must defend itself.'[36]

As such measures could only contrive to put the Front national in a stronger position for the elections of the following year, one might have expected Marine Le Pen to concentrate all her firepower on terrorism and immigration as that campaign developed. But the weight of the historical question of national identity proved unavoidable. Asked in a TV interview on 9 April 2017 about her manifesto's commitment to 'refusal of repentance', she literally returned to the Nazi era, rejecting Jacques Chirac's historic 1995 acceptance of national responsibility for the fate of more than thirteen thousand Jewish people rounded up and sent to their deaths in 1942:

I think that, generally, more generally, if there were those responsible, it was those in power at the time, it was not

France. France has been roughly handled in thinking about this for years. In reality, our children have been taught that they had many reasons to criticise her. To see perhaps only the darkest historical aspects. I want them to be proud of being French again.[37]

The history of views on this event, known as the Vel d'Hiv after the indoor cycle track where victims were herded, and commemorated annually on 16 July, demonstrates France's ongoing collective problem with its history of fascism and national identity. Until 1995, the official position of governments of all stripes was that articulated by De Gaulle upon the Liberation: Vichy was not France, France was the Republic, and the Republic had been elsewhere during those dark years. One place it had been, notably, was in Central Africa, one of the first regions of the empire to declare for the Free French. This was another reason why it pained the French establishment to consider confronting imperialism as a crime.

In September 1994, President François Mitterrand had reaffirmed his stance against accepting the guilt of Vichy crimes starkly and publicly: 'I will not apologise in the name of France. The Republic had nothing to do with this. I do not believe France is responsible.' Mitterrand, who had been a Vichy civil servant while building a career-enhancing resistance record, and who maintained a personal friendship with Vichy police chief René Bousquet into the 1980s (as well as serving in some of the governments that had fought the Algerian War), had his own complex reasons for blocking contemplation of these events. Bousquet, who had played a significant part in them, was assassinated in 1993 while awaiting trial for his involvement.[38]

Chirac's speech at the 1995 Vel d'Hiv commemoration, coming weeks after he assumed office, marked a generational repudiation of the postwar politics that had seen Vichy officials, after often token punishments, enjoy long careers in national and imperial administration, while Vichy itself was pushed away as an alien entity.[39] He pulled no punches in assuming responsibility: 'France, the homeland of the Enlightenment and of the rights of man, a land of welcome and asylum, on that day committed the irreparable. Breaking its word, it handed those who were under its protection over to their executioners.' Such 'dark hours forever sully our history' and an 'everlasting debt' to the victims remained.

Seventeen years later, marking the seventieth anniversary of the events shortly after his own election, President François Hollande reaffirmed this message, singling out the 'lucidity and courage' with which Chirac had confronted the issue. In his speech he insisted that 'the dark hours of the collaboration' were part of 'our history and therefore of France's responsibility':

> The truth is hard, cruel. The truth is that the French police arrested thousands of children and families. Not one German soldier was mobilised for this operation. The truth is, this was a crime committed in France, by France.[40]

This is what Marine Le Pen sought to put aside – not, perhaps, for the same reasons her father would have rejected the sentiment, and certainly not for the entangled reasons that haunted the Mitterrand generation.[41] After her interview she nonetheless demonstrated that this whole history remained live, referencing it in a written statement:

> Like Charles de Gaulle [and] François Mitterrand... I consider that France and the Republic were in London during the Occupation and that the Vichy regime was not France. This is a position that was always defended by the head of state, prior to Jacques Chirac and above all François Hollande going back on it, wrongly.

In pushing Vichy and its crime back into the 'grey zone' of an 'illegal collaborator regime', Le Pen sought the mantle of the 'true' history of a Republic that was innocent of any crime, and the credit for saving it from recent, passing errors. Her efforts lost out to the rise of Emmanuel Macron, who followed in the tradition of Chirac and Hollande in July 2017, making his own speech in which he hardened still further the line of responsibility:

> Just recently, what we considered to be established by the authorities of the French Republic across party lines, proven by all historians and confirmed by the national conscience, was contested by French political leaders prepared to trample on the truth. Responding to these counterfeiters is to do them too much honour, but to leave them unanswered would be worse, making us accomplices.
>
> So yes, I will say this here: it is France that organised the round-up, subsequent deportation and, consequently, for almost all of them, the death of the 13,152 French Jews dragged from their homes on July 16 and 17 1942.[42]

After a minute's silence, he went on: 'I condemn all the tricks and subtleties of those who claim today that Vichy was not France'; he then named the leading officials, including Bousquet, who were involved, and embraced the need to move on from the silence of De Gaulle's and Mitterrand's generation. Allowing for the honourable and glorious record of the resistance, it was nonetheless unacceptable to put Vichy aside:

> It is easy to view Vichy as a monstrosity that grew out of nothing and returned to nothingness, to believe that these people came out of nowhere and received just punishment at the liberation that eliminated them from the national community. It is easy, so easy... but it is wrong. And no pride can be built on a lie.

From there he launched into a searing account of the fate of the deportees, the responsibility of the society that had allowed the toxins of racism and antisemitism to spread unchecked through its veins, and of the duty of the present day to remember and to pledge itself never to permit such things again.

But there is a twist in this ending, because little more than hours after Macron spoke, Jean-Luc Mélenchon, star leader of the far-left movement La France insoumise, published a lengthy denunciation of the speech on his personal blog. Beginning with a conventional leftist attack on the presence of the 'extreme right' Israeli Prime Minister Netanyahu at the ceremony, and on Macron's linkage of antisemitism with anti-Zionism, Mélenchon segued into the claim that 'to declare that France is responsible for the Vel d'Hiv round-up is to cross a threshold of maximal intensity'. Acting as if the history of this event since 1995 simply did not exist, he asserted that 'to say that France, as a people, as a nation is responsible for this crime is to deploy a completely unacceptable essentialist definition of our country'. Yet his very next sentence was 'France is nothing except our Republic' – which, he declared, of course, 'was in London with General de Gaulle'. Mélenchon then went on to demonstrate that he was quite adept at creating essentialist definitions when it suited him:

> By its resistance, its combat against the invaders and by the re-establishment of the Republic once they had been chased from the territory, the French people proved which side it was really on. It is not in Monsieur Macron's power to assign all the French the identity of hangmen which is not theirs! No, no, Vichy is not France![43]

Between them, Marine Le Pen and Jean-Luc Mélenchon won almost 41 per cent of the votes in the first round of the 2017 presidential election – 14.7 million compared to the 8.6 million who put Macron first. The problem France has with its historical identity is a profound one indeed.

5
Who Do They Think We Are?

It used to be fairly clearly the case that problems of historical identity rarely troubled the collective British mind. In recent decades the tide of nationalism following on from devolution has altered this for some. Nonetheless, the pungent comment that Salman Rushdie in 1988 put into the stuttering mouth of a character in *The Satanic Verses* has mostly remained true: 'The trouble with the English is that their history happened overseas, so they don't know what it means.'[1] Analysis of the vote for Brexit, and the opinions generated in its wake, suggests that 'the English' remain befuddled about the implications of the history they are making, and increasingly dangerously angry about what they don't understand.

Perhaps grimmest of all were the responses in December 2016, when YouGov asked voters why they thought the other side had voted.[2] Forty-three per cent of Leave voters attributed a Remain vote to fear of change, four times more than any other response (7 per cent said it was plain stupidity). For Remain voters thinking about Leavers' motivations, 'immigration' topped the list at 43 per cent, followed by racism, misinformation and stupidity at around 10 per cent each. In a word-cloud of associated responses, the single word 'immigration' loomed so large as to make other responses literally indecipherable. Only 8 per cent of Remain voters mentioned sovereignty. Twenty-three per cent of younger Remain voters highlighted racism as an explanation.

Eight months later, two polls released within hours of each other showed both the confusion and the bitterness of the public, as the government continued to give out contradictory messages about exit negotiations that had not properly begun. ComRes reported that voters as a whole prioritised access to EU markets over restrictions on free movement to reduce immigration by two to one. What appeared to be government policy – exiting the single market to end free movement – was supported by only 26 per cent. Asked what they thought should happen to EU citizens currently resident in the UK, a comforting 69 per cent thought they should not be forced out, but 27 per cent thought some should go and 10 per cent that most should. Just under a fifth of those in the lowest income categories favoured mass expulsion.[3]

This grimmer note was echoed in a poll by YouGov of self-professed Leave voters. Sixty-one per cent of them agreed with the statement that 'significant damage to the British economy would be a price worth paying for bringing Britain out of the EU'. A majority in every age group over twenty-five shared this sentiment, rising to 70 per cent among the over-sixty-fives. Among Leavers overall, 39 per cent also agreed that losing their job, or the job of a family member, would be a price worth paying, a figure that rose to 50 per cent among the over-sixty-fives. Putting a similar question to Remain voters showed that around 20 per cent would be willing for similar things to happen to 'teach Leave politicians and Leave voters a lesson'.[4]

Further analysis of the referendum results, and of people's reactions to them, continues to produce a fascinating, if dispiriting, picture of British life. A report by the Joseph Rowntree Foundation pulled no punches in highlighting poverty and lack of opportunity within the UK population as a key cause of Brexit sympathies: 'Groups in Britain who have been "left behind" by rapid economic change and feel cut adrift from the mainstream consensus were the most likely to support Brexit.' The Foundation emphasised that these outcomes were the results of processes of increasing deprivation and marginalisation caused by government economic and educational policies, and not merely static facts. Where there had been a sudden jolt of immigration into deprived communities, the resentments sharpened the Brexit response.[5]

This can be paralleled by the widely reported preference for Leave of older voters, and those of lower social classes generally.[6] In such responses, and the patent incapacity of anyone in the political class to turn the majority away from the perception that loss of status is somehow the fault of foreigners, there is a grim echo of Orwell's concern about a working class that might turn its self-perception as 'downtrodden slaves' into a desire to carry on benefiting from 'colonial exploitation'. There can of course be no simple correlation of social class with opinion on this matter – the 'DE' semi-skilled and unskilled categories only make up a little over a quarter of the population, and at the other end the 'AB' professional and managerial classes slightly less. Necessarily, most voters on either side sat somewhere in the middle.[7] Nevertheless, social and cultural divisions framed by tensions around poverty and education show up again and again in other analyses.

In February 2017, the BBC reported on a detailed evaluation of voting results in the Brexit referendum, covering over half of the UK.[8] The area reporting the highest vote for Leave, 82.5 per cent, was Brambles and Thorntree, a deprived estate in east Middlesbrough.[9] According to the local council, this area has the lowest proportion of residents with a higher-education qualification in England and Wales, at 4 per cent. The ward reporting the highest vote for Remain, at 87.8 per cent, was Market, central Cambridge, home to the university. Such almost parodically apt results were the extremes of a very clear national pattern. A broader analysis of voting by ward showed a clustering of the huge majority of results along an almost-straight line from high-Leave, low-qualification to high-Remain, high-qualification areas.

A major investigation by the NatCen social-research charity added further layers.[10] Almost 70 per cent of those who rented their housing from a local authority or housing association were Leave voters, while a narrow majority of private renters and homeowners were for Remain. There was also strong evidence of the impact of the politically polarised and socially divided market for national newspapers: 70 per cent of those who regularly read the *Sun* or the *Daily Express* voted Leave, as did 66 per cent of *Daily Mail* readers. Intriguingly, the *Daily Mirror*, which appeals to the same demographics as the *Sun* but leans towards Labour, saw 56 per cent of its readers vote Remain. In the broadsheet market, 55 per cent of *Telegraph* readers were for Leave but only 30 per cent of *Times* readers, 22 per cent for the *Financial Times* and an intriguing 9 per cent of *Guardian* readers, presumably the 'Lexiteers'. An unsurprising 98 per cent of those who identified as UKIP voters were for Leave, along with 58 per cent of Tory voters (despite the official Remain stance of their party); Labour-identifying voters voted for Remain by more than 60 per cent, as did those of other parties. Tellingly, individuals who rejected identification with any party voted Leave by 70 per cent.[11]

At one level, all of this is unsurprising. The British population has been opposed to increased immigration, by quite substantial majorities, since polling on the subject began in the postwar decades. A study by the Oxford University Migration Observatory, published in 2011, showed that graduates were the only group where a majority disagreed with the statement that immigration should be reduced 'a lot', and three-quarters of those who had never managed a C-grade at GCSE agreed with it. The same sentiment earned majorities of 60+ per cent among all groups with annual incomes below £20,000, and only those earning £75,000+ disapproved of it by a substantial majority. In literally every region except London, overall majorities for a serious reduction in immigration ran at more than 80 per cent, and even in London reached 68 per cent.[12] It will also always be worth recalling that 'free movement', as defined by the EU single market, actually included provision for significant regulation, and a much closer watch on individual workers could have been kept. It was decisions by UK governments – Labour and then a Tory/LibDem coalition – not to bother enforcing this that fuelled the fears of 'uncontrolled' migration over the last decade.[13]

The argument around all this continues nonetheless, and demonstrates the continuing unwillingness of those who promoted Brexit most fiercely to admit what poll after poll shows the public really thought. Over a year after the vote, Daniel Hannan, a Conservative MEP unyieldingly devoted to 'reclaiming' British national sovereignty, could be found in the pages of the *New York Times* hymning liberated Britain's rising prosperity, claiming that it is only Remainers who think the vote was about immigration, and lambasting 'a few Euro-fanatics, disproportionately prominent on the BBC and at the *Financial Times*... acting like doomsday cultists'.[14] It is as if Nigel Farage had not warned, in early June 2016, of mass sex attacks by immigrants if Britain remained in the EU,[15] and had not produced – and been depicted across the media standing in front of – a poster of a stream of immigrants (in fact Syrian refugees in Central Europe) with the tagline 'Breaking Point' and a demand to 'take back control'.[16]

Hours before the referendum polls opened, a *Washington Post* report summed up the stream of racist stereotypes and neo-Nazi infiltration visible within the Leave campaign and its social-media presence as 'ripples of bigoted glee' at the unleashing of the previously unsayable into the public mainstream.[17] In the weeks after the vote, reported racial hate crimes doubled and in some cases tripled in the areas with heaviest Leave votes.[18] Jo Cox, of course, had already paid for her public stance against such bigotry with her life.

Even before the Brexit vote, it was already commonplace to connect the rise of Farage with the concurrent looming rise of Trump, and both to the exploitation of sentiments that may have been unpleasant in their 'nativism' but also understandable responses to social marginalisation under globalising neoliberalism.[19] At the leftist fringe of this, the online journal of the Socialist Workers Party quoted Lenin's view that revolution was inconceivable 'without revolutionary outbursts by a section of the petty bourgeoisie with all its prejudices, without a movement of the politically non-conscious proletarian and semi-proletarian masses' that had to be taken as it was found and bent to the will of good Marxists. This meant putting aside 'fears' about racism, and embracing the 'bitter anger at the grinding and relentless attacks on working-class people since the onset of the financial crisis' that lay, allegedly, beneath the surface of Trump's and Farage's popular support.[20] Jeremy Corbyn, in leaping to accept the Brexit verdict and the 'freedom to shape our economy for the future' it supposedly gave, also proclaimed solidarity with the millions who 'feel shut out of a political and economic system that has let them down', and who had given 'one clear message' about this in voting Leave.[21] Labour frontbenchers have continued to deny the salience of anti-immigrant sentiment into 2017.[22]

We are thus faced with the spectacle of a majority of the poorest sections of society willingly accepting a future of increased poverty in order to escape an institution that they blame for allowing in immigrants to take people's jobs. Such an outcome was forecast with absolute clarity by the UK Treasury's official pre-referendum analysis in April 2016. This predicted that, fifteen years after Brexit, the best-case scenario of a 'Norway-like' relationship would see the UK's annual GDP almost 4 per cent lower than it would otherwise have been, and in the worst-case, hardest Brexit, some 7.5 per cent lower – an annual cost to each household of more than £5,000.[23] Such figures were of course drawn up by experts, of whom, as Michael Gove noted in June 2016, the British public has 'had enough'.[24] He was still repeating that assertion ten months later, while also refusing to give up on the idea, long discredited by expert opinion, that one day the NHS would get the extra £350 million a week the Leave campaign had promised.[25]

While public views around Brexit look very much like a country tearing itself apart out of pure spite, the rise of Marine Le Pen in France has exposed bitter discontent across the French cultural landscape. Not least of the disturbing messages of her success is that, while younger people in Britain are currently rallying to Jeremy Corbyn's Labour in great numbers, there is nothing to suggest that a few years of unsuccessful social democracy in a context of Brexit-induced economic decline could not turn them sharply rightwards.

Support for Le Pen's policies – smashing the EU's 'globalist' grip and persecuting immigrants and minorities in the name of 'law and order', while promising 'real' French people the economic comforts of *les Trente Glorieuses* – is not centred among the old.[26] The first round of the 2017 presidential poll bore this out, with 45 per cent of voters aged seventy+ choosing the traditionalist conservative Fillon and only 10 per cent Le Pen. However, she came second to Mélenchon's rebellious appeal among the under-twenty-fives and topped the poll among thirty-five-to fifty-nine-year-olds.[27]

In the second round of voting, with a straight fight between Le Pen and Macron (and one-third of voters abstaining or spoiling their ballots), Le Pen's vote showed a similar profile, from lows of 34 per cent for the under-twenty-fives and 22 per cent for the over-seventies to a peak of 43 per cent among the thirty-five to forty-nines.[28] More telling still was the social profile that emerged. While Macron unsurprisingly took 82 per cent of the votes of managers and professionals, and 74 per cent of those who had made it to retirement, Le Pen claimed 46 per cent of non-manual *employés* and a substantial 56 per cent of those calling themselves 'workers'.

Prior to the campaign, it was widely reported that Le Pen was polling as high as 40 per cent among younger age groups, and that this was a sign of her successful de-demonisation of the FN, particularly among those with no direct experience of her father's outbursts.[29] Persistent high youth unemployment, and a sclerotic political system that repeatedly failed to deliver promised reforms to address this, were other parts of the picture. Conscious efforts by the FN to present a youthful image, filling their rallies with smartly dressed party members in their twenties, and the election of Marion Maréchal-Le Pen, Marine's niece, as the country's youngest MP, enhanced this appeal. Some 20 per cent of local FN officials are under thirty-five, contrasting sharply (until the sudden emergence of Macron) with the often geriatric image of the mainstream parties.[30]

Other studies have noted that the FN's long presence in French politics is now having a generational effect, and that almost 80 per cent of its youngest supporters have parents who are supporters of the party and have passed on this engagement with anti-system beliefs.[31] While only 30 per cent of this group came from the 'popular classes', almost 70 per cent declared themselves Catholic – suggesting that cultural conservatism remains an important factor in their politics. In a finding that is much more obviously of the moment, two-thirds of these young FN supporters (and more than three-quarters of those holding party office) said that they trust the internet for their political news, against only 24 per cent the television and a paltry 19 per cent the national press.

The rise of politics among younger groups that embraces new technology and the targeting of messages has enabled the FN to cross some boundaries that at first sight seem implausible. Relentless campaigning against the perceived alien dogmas of Islam appears to have won Le Pen a solid following among France's younger gay population. Many gay men, alarmed about violent homophobia, side with the FN's defence of republican values – and some, indeed, occupy important party offices. A poll in May 2017 suggested that 35 per cent of gay men in their thirties and forties intended to vote for Le Pen as president, and 45 per cent of those under thirty.[32] This preference manages to coexist with the party's hostility to other measures such as equal marriage (introduced to France only in 2013 and vocally opposed by, for example, Marion Maréchal-Le Pen).[33] As a BBC report noted, at least some prosperous gay white men treat such positions as 'a bluff: a ploy to win conservative votes', choosing to take those FN policies they agree with as more real.[34] A black DJ interviewed for the same report commented caustically on the 'very selfish' attitudes of some who 'feel like they're not targets for the FN any more so they think it's OK to vote for them'.

At the same time as some may have taken a sanitised FN at its word, it remains associated with a dimension of youth mobilisation that is explicitly hostile not merely to Islam but to all multiculturalism and to the physical presence of refugees and migrants. A group calling itself 'Génération Identitaire' claims a six-figure number of social-media supporters and has carried out stunts, including protests demanding the closure of refugee camps, and an apparent attempt to prevent the rescue of migrants from the Mediterranean. The demands of such groups return to the classic extreme-right agendas of mass deportation of ethnic minorities.[35] Although FN activists in public restrict themselves to acceptable slogans such as 'economic patriotism' and 'self-determination' in describing policies that would take France out of the EU and into a protectionist realm, commentators report that the official FN policy 'to exclude anyone uttering openly racist comments' is limited to high-profile cases, and that tacit acceptance of such views is prevalent.[36] The distance between ethnic nationalism and the widely shared view that 'For us, 1,500 years of history isn't nothing' is narrow.[37]

One of the disheartening things about the continued rise of the FN is the huge number of real problems they offer to solve with their solipsistic and ultimately doomed form of nationalism. France does have a paralysingly unequal economy, with entrenched long-term unemployment and massive regional imbalances. Much of its north-eastern third is on the way to becoming a post-industrial wasteland (where votes for Le Pen regularly top 40 per cent), while many of its beautiful and historic regional towns – Albi, Agen, Limoges, Bourges, Arras, Béziers, Auxerre, Vichy, Calais – have been gutted by out-of-town developments and generational migration, becoming little more than empty stage sets for wandering tourists. This problem is so damaging to local pride that those trying to expose it have had to work in semi-secrecy, denounced as alien intruders.[38]

Similar portraits – though perhaps without the tourists – could be painted of the many areas of northern England where more than half of voters opted to leave the EU. Recipients of government largesse in the New Labour years (and not a little European regional support funding), these areas saw millions 'lifted out of poverty' by Gordon Brown's redistributive schemes. These turned out to be umbilically connected to the massive consumer-credit and house-price bubble that Brown's banking deregulation had engineered, and lacking in any self-sustaining economic impact that could have saved people from crashing back into poverty on a change of government.

Although in an immediate sense the impact of austerity after 2010 has been dire, the failure to offer actual structural change that would regenerate post-industrial regions and create meaningful prosperity for their inhabitants is the fault of governments, both Labour and Conservative, stretching back for at least a generation. A similar picture of long-term abandonment to the tender mercies of the laissez-faire marketplace is of course evident across the American Midwest, where it tipped the balance of victory for Donald Trump.

Such areas have seen the re-emergence of a fringe of the violent far-right. A motley array of groups can now be found, often latching on to what they claim are obvious connections between Muslim immigration and Islamist terrorism to project themselves as defenders of the nation. In Britain, with a few tragic exceptions, such groups have rarely risen to the level of a serious threat. In the USA, however, there have been on average around three deadly attacks every year by right-wing extremists since the turn of the century, killing almost fifty people up to 2016 – more than have died in other forms of terrorism since the events of 11 September 2001.[39] Non-fatal right-wing violence ran at five or six incidents a week, and less-violent incidents – harassment, graffiti, threatening notes – at several dozen a week. Immediately after the election of Donald Trump, the Southern Poverty Law Center reported that these spiked to almost a hundred a day. Antisemitic incidents in early 2017 were reportedly running at almost double the rate of the year before.[40]

Since the 1980s, with Ronald Reagan's campaign rhetoric of black 'welfare queens' leeching off the taxpayer, the Republican Party has associated its small-government agenda with race. The resentments of white voters who perceive themselves as less well-off (but only sometimes are) have become one of the main engines of partisanship in US politics. As late as the mid-1990s, Bill Clinton's brand of Southern-inflected Democrat politics secured majorities in states from Louisiana to Kentucky; since 2000 that vote has plunged below 40 per cent. That shift is associated with another one, as the Republican vote has piled up higher and higher in states with lower average educational attainment. In 1992 there was almost no statistical relationship between those two things, but by 2012 Republicans dominated the vote in states with low graduate populations, by up to 70 per cent.[41]

This shift in partisan allegiance has been accompanied by disturbing trends in other, related attitudes. Long-term polling on Republican voters' attitudes to 'blacks' showed a slow but steady rise in positive sentiments from the 1960s to around 2004. Since then it has plummeted by more than ten percentage points, on what appears to be an accelerating curve. There are clear indications that 'old-fashioned racism' returned to political prominence as white voters struggled to deal with the reality of a black president.[42] As well as attitudes to the African-American population, approaches to immigration reflected both uncertainty and prejudice. Trump's barnstorming promise to simply wall off the USA from the south responded to the fact that, in the preceding quarter-century, the foreign-born population had almost doubled to 13.9 per cent. The last time that happened, a century earlier, the nativist backlash had virtually closed the US to immigration for several decades (including for the many Jews attempting to flee Hitler's Europe who were denied visas).[43]

The recent wave of new immigration, partly due to the changing availability of work, has spread itself far beyond those states accustomed to seeing a regular influx of new-comers. The political consequences were starkly obvious in the 2012 election. Almost every state with a significant long-term immigrant population voted for Obama, and almost all of them had seen growth in that population of less than 100 per cent in the previous two decades. Almost every state without such a long-term population voted for Romney in 2012, and thirteen of these had seen the immigrant population rise since 1990 by more than 150 per cent. In six cases – Georgia, Nebraska, Kentucky, Tennessee, Arkansas and North Carolina – that increase was around 300 per cent. Meanwhile, the curve of declining Republican sentiment about blacks has also been matched by a similar ten-point slide in feelings about Hispanics.[44]

It has been easy to focus on the extent to which the 'Trump voter' is a man or woman who feels under economic threat – an actually marginalised, relatively poor, older, less-educated victim of structural economic change.[45] It is certainly true that there were enough such people, particularly in the Rustbelt Midwest, to tip the balance of the election. But as with the presence of such figures in the earlier Tea Party movement, they were the tip of a much larger iceberg of privilege. The long-term history of the racist right in America demonstrates a firm grounding in the middle and upper classes.[46] Most of those who turned out to vote for Trump in the Republican primaries earned well above the median US household income.[47]

That median income is itself racially divided. A 2015 study showed that black and Hispanic households possessed only a tiny fraction, 6–8 per cent, of the average net wealth of white households.[48] A 2016 study demonstrated that the income gap between black and white households had barely narrowed since the 1960s, with whites bringing in on average some $63,000, and blacks less than $37,000 annually. At the upper end of the educational scale the problem is not static, but worsening. Black male college graduates in the 1980s started their careers earning about 10 per cent less than their white peers; that figure is now 18 per cent. Black and white female college graduates earned roughly the same in the early 1980s, but in the last thirty-five years the income of Black women has fallen back by 12 per cent. A narrowing gender wage gap has benefited white women almost exclusively.[49]

Against this background, right-wing groups have long campaigned on the fantastical proposition that 'Affirmative Action', an umbrella term for various initiatives to combat racial and other prejudices in the educational and employment spheres, was giving black people in particular an unfair advantage over 'deserving' whites. The idea that white people faced discrimination in the current social and legal system was a conviction, and a profound concern, for core Trump voters.[50] In 2013, and again in 2016, a white woman from Texas took a case all the way to the Supreme Court, arguing that her failure to get into a prestigious university was a consequence of the application of Affirmative Action to other, non-white, applicants who did not deserve it. She lost, and factual evidence shows plainly that, as a group, white women were the dominant beneficiaries of Affirmative Action over the past thirty years.[51]

Nonetheless, attitudes hardened as Trump's fortunes rose. At the start of 2016, 53 per cent of Republican voters already thought the USA had done enough for racial equality; by the end of the year that number rose to 62 per cent. In contrast, only 10 per cent of blacks agreed.[52] It was predictable that in the summer of 2017 the US Justice Department began realigning its civil-rights division to attack Affirmative Action, making internal plans for 'investigations and possible litigation related to intentional race-based discrimination in college and university admissions'.[53] Scathing retorts, noting for example that a white high-school dropout still has roughly the same job prospects as a black college graduate, or that 'legacy admissions' of previous graduates' relatives continue to get hundreds of under-qualified white people into elite colleges, will have little effect on those committed to this path.[54]

Such views accompany the other widespread myth of voting fraud by non-white populations, which helped to hound the voter-registration charity ACORN out of existence in 2010 and persists as a key belief of Trump supporters – and of Trump himself, who has claimed that such fraud robbed him of victory in the popular-vote tally.[55] A poll in August 2017 even suggested that half of Republican voters would agree to postponing the 2020 election to ensure 'only eligible voters participated'.[56] Not even the Second World War, or the Civil War, ever delayed a US presidential election, and there is absolutely no evidence of meaningful levels of such fraud.[57] The evidence that local Republican politicians systematically set out to make voting difficult-to-impossible for minority groups is overwhelming, however.[58]

Social scientists, pollsters and journalists have all documented the pervasive feeling among right-leaning white Americans that others are 'stealing their place in line', getting ahead 'at the expense of white men and their wives'. By late 2015, almost two-thirds of Republican voters thought that 'discrimination against whites' was a problem as large as any other discrimination, and for Trump supporters a key component of their general economic anxiety was a sentiment of racial decline: 'I think minorities are taking jobs from people like me.'[59] Similar beliefs are widespread in Britain, notably the contradictory conviction that 'immigrants' simultaneously steal jobs and enjoy generous welfare benefits and free housing (at a time when all such benefits are being cut back rigorously, driving many into destitution). And, just as Trump supporters are untouched by factual evidence, so in Britain the practice of lengthy detention and routine deportation of asylum seekers makes no mark on such preconceptions.

The logic that drives the Trump movement is one of racial prejudice and racial privilege, in which both new immigrants and the African-American descendants of slaves are not 'real' Americans and represent a threat to those who are. How else to explain the assertion that Black Lives Matter, a protest movement born out of desperation at witnessing a stream of unpunished murders of black men by law-enforcement officers, was in fact a 'terrorist' organisation and a threat to national security?[60] It ties neatly back to the quoted (and unfortunately typical) remark of one Trump supporter during the campaign: 'I feel he's the last chance we have to establish law and order and preserve the culture I grew up in.'[61]

The extent to which that culture depends on a violent exercise of racial domination was exposed in a 2017 book by the broadcast journalist Chris Hayes. Entitled bluntly *A Colony in a Nation*, it describes a society in which the dominant white population lives with the best standards of safety and security in the world while the black and other minority population is almost literally held down by militarised policing, prejudicial local laws and a massive, industrialised prison system. Established, perpetuated and enforced by the democratic will of the majority, this is the heritage of a society literally built on slavery.[62] And, like slavery in earlier centuries, one of the forces that drives it to greater excesses is the terror of imagining what would happen if the oppressed broke free. Mining that terror, and using it to stoke the fires of political disruption, is a vast political industry in the USA. In that context, the excitement of a fringe of fascistic white-supremacist groups at Trump's election is less significant than the real everyday oppression of those they claim to be oppressed by.[63]

6

What is the Past For?

Is there a route to salvation from our demented relationship with the past? In August 2017, the historian Christopher Kissane, a 'BBC/AHRC New Generation Thinker', boldly proposed that 'Historical research and analysis is a seditious rejection of those who seek to control the past in order to shape the future', and historians should stand up for its public role as such:

> History should not appear only on screen or in print for antiquarian appeal or provocation, but to inform wider debates. Like economics and science, historical expertise has a place in the analysis of current affairs, and indeed in the assessment of politics and policy. Historians must also take it upon ourselves to increase our engagement with broader audiences, spreading awareness of the content, diversity and importance of our work. This change must extend, too, to the education of the next generation: in

schools, history should sit alongside languages, science and maths as core subjects for every child.[1]

The bitter irony of such a list is that, in fact, many of these good things already happen. History is, and has always been, one of the core subjects of the English National Curriculum. Since 2002, the dedicated historians who run the History & Policy group have systematically engaged policy makers in the UK with historical evidence.[2] It is true that the 'stars' of television history broadcasting can be counted on one's fingers, and some of them are not even professional historians, but the very competition Kissane had won exists to address that problem.

The sticking point is that this proposal hinges on the idea of a simple deficit, persisting despite decades of educational effort. The young British poet and rapper Akala made a very similar point in an impassioned speech in May 2017, exploring 'the battle of Britishness in the age of Brexit' and concluding: 'the answer is education. Confrontation with difficult histories and developing an understanding of how those histories have shaped the present.'[3] In both these well-intentioned interventions, the problem is defined as a lack of enough good historical work out there, telling people how it really was, overcoming ignorance with facts. But there are entire bookshops' worth of good historical work, whole departments of bold young historians (and some grizzled old veterans) who have been telling their students, and anyone else who would listen, how it really was for at least a generation. The problem remains what to do when people don't want to listen, or learn.

Historians constantly address the value of their studies for wider society. Ludmilla Jordanova's *History in Practice*, in its first edition, ends with a 'Postscript: History's future: a personal statement', which despite its proclaimed individuality could stand for many such contributions: differences in practice are good, as long as there are underlying standards of scrupulous research; passionate commitment can be balanced with probing detachment. 'In both their teaching and their research, historians should, responsibly, unsettle their audiences, provoke them to think harder and deeper about the human condition.'[4] In the following pages she presses the case for historians to be more systematically engaged in 'public history' in its various forms, including its controversies, to think of themselves as 'bearing witness', notably for those in the past whose voices would otherwise remain silenced, and to 'stand firmly in the present as mediators between past and future'. All this with integrity, transparency, rigour and a commitment to widening understanding of every part of the historical process.[5]

At the turn of the century, when that first edition appeared, a cautious optimism about all of those things was still plausible. Six years later, in a second edition, caution began to outweigh optimism. Opening with the explicit impact of '9/11', this new postscript mused on the role of topics like military history and the study of the Holocaust in 'the current war-torn state of the world'.[6] Discussing the variously porous boundaries between academic and public histories, Jordanova suggests that 'Perhaps more attention should be paid to why the past is used so little and highly selectively, why it is deployed so badly in making decisions and forming opinions.'[7] Although she ends with a version of her previous sentiments, the tone of her closing paragraph is far more uncertain: while 'the marketability of history' should spur new reflections from 'self-aware and intellectually robust' practitioners, 'It would be a shame' if this displaced 'the doing of history'. In the very last few lines, the risk from 'blockbuster films and books that retell familiar stories' continues to intrude into the prospects for a discipline that 'will indeed thrive from openness and diversity… honest toil, analytical self-awareness and excellent writing'.[8]

There is an unavoidable sense here that a further burden has fallen from the wider world on to the shoulders of historians, even between these two editions, and that the mission to improve the world through greater knowledge of the past has grown more difficult. How much more difficult, and indeed tormented, it is now felt to be shows up if we place Jordanova alongside the vision that E. H. Carr articulated in *What is History?*, first published in 1961. Produced as a Penguin paperback in 1964, it was reprinted almost every year until a 'second edition' appeared in 1987, which was the same text with the addition of a short new preface. The essentially unchanged 1961 text is still in print today. Its lasting significance is signalled by its central place, under 'The Uses of Facts', as a reading exercise on the University of Cambridge website aimed at prospective history undergraduates.[9] It is almost certainly no exaggeration to say that anyone who has touched on the fringes of historical methodologies in the last fifty years is more likely to have read Carr's book than any other. And in that context the vision of the historian's mission it articulates, while very much of its original time, is now quite extraordinary.

Carr starts out by framing history, reasonably enough, as an active process of writing. The first chapter neatly skewers the idea that some things are 'historical facts' by their very nature, highlighting the need for decisions about significance – essentially selective decisions, driven by historians' concepts and preferences – that precede the elevation of any mere piece of information to the status of a fact. The second chapter insists that individuals, even 'great men', cannot be treated outside their social context and that history is a particular way of measuring the value of that context, a dialogue between past and present, furthering the better understanding of both.

From here Carr becomes ever-more pointedly prescriptive. The third chapter argues for history to sit alongside the sciences and social sciences, rather than more humanistic pursuits, and the fourth amplifies this point with the case for history as a study of what it is useful to know about what caused events in the past. Already implicitly breaking the boundary between the academic and the publicly political, Carr turns inexorably towards the future, and in his fifth chapter puts that usefulness to work by espousing an unambiguous belief in real, generalised progress. Indeed, he goes so far as to declare that 'History properly so-called can be written only by those who find and accept a sense of direction in history itself', and that 'A society which has lost belief in its capacity to progress in the future' will soon abandon history.[10]

In the sixth and final chapter – which one must suspect relatively few of the many, many students assigned this text to read ever reached – Carr roundly denounces all varieties of intellectual pessimism in favour of full-throated commitment to modernity as a progressive global undertaking, driven forward by the combined forces of Marx, Freud and advancing technology.[11] Lauding 'the bold readiness of human beings not to confine themselves to seeking piecemeal improvements... but to present fundamental challenges in the name of reason to the current way of doing things', Carr emphatically looks forward to a future in which Anglophone scholars 'regain their courage for that task'. The risk of not doing so, he avers, is 'that this country... may lag behind the general advance, and relapse helplessly and uncomplainingly into some nostalgic backwater'.[12]

If it comes as a shock to discover that the E. H. Carr who sits fossilised at the head of so many introductory reading lists was a revolutionary Marxist, then it is worth also noting that others of his generation now often seen as soft centrists could say very similar things. J. H. Plumb's 1969 text, *The Death of the Past*, which, like Carr's, remains in print today, sought to elevate the practice of history above the ways in which states and cultures had previously used the past to justify the present and prefigure the future. As with Carr's aspirations, Plumb's goals tended towards the hubristic and the tautological.

He was keen to note how 'The critical historical process' weakened 'the past', understood as 'those simple, structural generalizations by which our forefathers interpreted the purpose of life in historical terms'. Yet he was equally certain that 'The majority of men and women... realise that they are part of an historical process that has changed over the centuries... that they require to know what the nature of this process has been and is. They need an historical past, objective and true.'[13]

In the final chapter of the book, Plumb insists that historians have a 'twofold purpose': to cultivate the detailed study of minute specialisms that provide the building-blocks of future understanding, and to reach out on the widest scale, 'reveal the complexities of human behaviour and the strangeness of events', and create a 'past serviceable to society' that promotes the 'one truth of history – that the condition of mankind has improved' and can be further perfected. Thus 'Historians can use history to fulfil many of the social purposes which the old mythical pasts did so well.'[14]

Both Carr and Plumb – men born before the First World War, still in print, still haunting reading-lists – reflect the cultural hangover of our Concorde-building era: the hubris of a still-small elite intellectual class in the first flush of the postwar baby-boom growth in students, convinced that it was within their power not just to chart a route to a better future via the past, but to actually direct, from their Oxbridge fellowships and chairs, the course of the nation towards that future.

Compared to the massive programmatic optimism of such writers, calls like those of Christopher Kissane lose their initial bold edge, coming to seem more like the plea of a Cassandra for any attention at all from wider society. As we saw with the Cecil Rhodes statue controversy, even some great names of progressive reputation are reluctant to acknowledge in practice what might be required to actually make a difference. Other great names – of which, in his own estimation at least, Niall Ferguson is certainly the greatest – remain able to maintain a global profile and institutional affiliations of the highest calibre (Harvard, Oxford and the Hoover Institution, all at once), while making arguments for the value of empire and the dynamic superiority of the West that would certainly not feature in Kissane's vision of what history should be teaching.

Such arguments nonetheless find a ready market for books, TV series and very expensive speaking engagements, as well as regular newspaper columns, which do at least offer the opportunity to judge the pontificatory talents of such writers in real time. It has been instructive to watch Niall Ferguson shift his position on Brexit. In April 2016 he played the tough geopolitical realist, joining a general consensus of experts in rubbishing the panglossian economic predictions of Brexiteers such as Daniel Hannan, and condemned such people as 'happy morons' blithely detached from reality. After the referendum, in early July, he declared that Brexit would 'hurt', mocked the backstabbing among the Tory leadership contenders, and compared events to both Munich and Suez as destabilising shocks to the political system (and in the same piece downplayed the possibility of a Trump victory).[15]

By December 2016, with Trump en route to the White House, Ferguson carried out a tactical withdrawal, declaring he had been 'wrong' about Brexit, but blaming 'doomladen projections' from the IMF and others for misleading him, and laying into a EU allegedly in a 'ferment', and about to swing violently rightwards.[16] Then, in late July 2017, with everything he had previously predicted, then denied, starting to come to pass – 'blithe' Brexiteer promises 'exposed as the tosh I and many others said they were' and a 'bungled' snap election mangling the political landscape – he presented a remarkably tasteless extended comparison with the Dunkirk evacuation, observing that 'the remaining EU member states have us at their mercy', but we had to fight on: 'this is not the time for second thoughts – any more than May 1940 was the time for peace talks'.[17]

While Ferguson has executed what British political journalism pungently calls a 'reverse ferret', David Starkey has parlayed his undoubtedly profound knowledge of Tudor politics, and his reputation as 'the rudest man in Britain', into a role which allows him to predict the future reputations of prime ministers, and repeatedly compare Brexit to Henry VIII's split with Rome. In March 2017 he boldly declared on the BBC's *Today* programme that opposition politicians were 'intolerably tedious' in their quailing at Brexit, and that both the English Reformation and the referendum vote were the products of a 'British people' who 'knew what they were doing'.[18] His remarkable ability to explain the events of the twenty-first century through his expertise in the sixteenth has been rewarded with a variety of high-profile engagements, such as one for the investment advisers Patron Capital at the end of the same month, when he spoke on 'Trump, Brexit: what next?', no doubt with his usual measured gravitas.[19] Like Ferguson, Starkey is of course an ornament of one of Britain's finest universities, although Ferguson has never been dropped from an advertising campaign for being 'aggressively racist', as Starkey was by Cambridge in late 2015.[20] This has clearly been no barrier to his continuing career in punditry.

In France, the collision between what kinds of history can gain a high media profile and what the historical profession feels should happen increasingly resembles a crisis in the latter's eyes. Fears for the future of history as a discipline have become rampant in the last decade, as right-wing forces began to rally around 'national identity' as an issue.[21] For many professional historians, the dangerous consequences of this are summed up in the opening passages of a recent polemic by the medievalist Nicolas Offenstadt:

> Today, manipulation of historical facts in the public arena, in the more-or-less clear service of xenophobic or reactionary ideologies, has ratcheted upwards. The combat directed by a fraction of the right has taken on a new dimension, unseen for thirty years, and particularly reaches the mass media: television series and *prime time* shows, the daily press, magazines. In this cultural offensive, history is used as a political weapon, and is mobilised against university historians, described as *bien pensants*, too intellectual and abstract... history has come into play in the construction of a 'national identity', leading to the promotion of a rigid national story with xenophobic tendencies.[22]

As this list, and the dramatic claims about it, show, this is a complex field, where the inconvenient fact of some kinds of history being popular crosses over with the question of how far views on it are promoted by a shadowy elite, and how far the power of the state is engaged with defining acceptable histories, and repressing others.

Modern France has a long history of legal declarations about historical facts. In 1990 the *loi Gayssot* criminalised Holocaust denial and in 2001 a law formally recognised the Armenian genocide of the 1910s as a fact over continuing Turkish protestations. That same year, the *loi Taubira* declared that historical slavery and the slave trade were 'crimes against humanity'. In sharp contrast, after a change of government, in 2005 a law offered formal recognition and 'gratitude' to French personnel who had fought in colonial wars and been repatriated to France.[23] For a year, until its formal abrogation, Article 4.1 of this law ordered that 'Scholastic programmes recognise in particular the positive role of the French presence overseas, notably in North Africa, and accord to the history and the sacrifices of the French Army combatants born in these territories the eminent place to which they have a right.'[24] Although this particular passage did not survive the immediate, and international, polemic it provoked, the idea of the 'positive role of colonialism' has dogged political attitudes to history over the last decade.

It has done so alongside the other key tendency mentioned by Offenstadt – an anxious amplification of discussion about what the French call the *récit national*, or sometimes even more strongly the *roman national*, a single narrative of national history that claims to unify, while romanticising an essentialised idea of the nation, often over both the short and the very long term. This accounts for the remarkable place of diatribes about early-medieval history in some recent disputes. A group of historians in 2013 published *Les historiens de garde* – the title an untranslatably scornful play on the French term for 'watchdogs' – which devoted the first three of its six chapters to Loràant Deutsch, a thirtysomething actor who had become a media star with his book, and later TV series, *Métronome*, another punning title for a historical tour of Paris aligned with the names of metro stops.

Over dozens of pages, Deutsch's version of medieval history was furiously denounced, alongside his media exposure (often as if this were in itself a conspiracy of the power elite) and the parallels and connections all this had with the political agenda of promoting 'national identity' launched by the post-2007 Sarkozy presidency, explicitly connected to solving the 'problems' of immigration and assimilation. Deutsch publicly positioned himself as a Catholic royalist – something that is, by default, associated with the reactionary right in France – and promoted an approach to history involving a deep and emotional connection with the distant past of places associated with a royal and Catholic France, with the goal of accepting this as the true long-term national identity. His critics charged that not only was this a stalking-horse for wider reactionary agendas but it also involved the wholesale propagation of mythical fabrications, notably about the continuity of Catholic worship and institutions in the distant past.[25]

The issue of national historical memory, who guards it and for what, exploded into political life in the 2017 French presidential campaign. During a marathon TV debate between eleven candidates in April, Emmanuel Macron was challenged from the audience by a schoolteacher for distorting history in a way that would 'fuel resentment among some young people who have difficulties feeling

French' – in other words, harming the prospects for a successful assimilation to 'Frenchness' of the implicitly non-white sections of the population.

What Macron had done, on a trip to Algeria in February, was to declare that France's colonial history 'was a crime against humanity' meriting reflection and apology.[26] For this, he received a furious backlash from groups representing the former Algerian settlers, and had in fact almost immediately issued a remarkable public apology in a speech in Toulon: 'I have received some distressing letters... I'm sorry for wounding you, causing pain. I did not want to offend you. I know your lives, your troubles, your sufferings... these are vivid memories and not merely history. These are lives.'[27]

The fact that Macron still came under attack two months later for his original proposition shows that his policy of equivocation on this subject was failing to work. A few months earlier still, in November 2016, the magazine *Le Point* had drawn from him a notable effort at balancing the supposedly positive and negative sides of colonialism on the head of a pin. Asked whether 'we should revisit the less glorious pages of our history' in thinking about the *roman national*, Macron replied:

> ... yes, in Algeria, there was torture, but also the emergence of a State, of wealth, of a middle class, that's the reality of colonisation. There were elements of civilisation and elements of barbarity. Why do I speak of a *roman*? Because the role of imagination is central, it's what links us. In a *roman*, there are always good and bad *histoires* [histories, but also stories].[28]

Macron's stance was met with scorn from the left, but also looked from the right like meaningless hesitancy before what they perceived, and had already articulated, as a national emergency. In August 2016, centre-right frontrunner François Fillon delivered a blistering speech against an education system that, he claimed, denigrated French history. For him, that history was a single unified narrative, 'fifteen centuries of history since the baptism of Clovis at Reims', and not to teach that story was 'giving up on French society'. There must instead be an 'apprenticeship of respect and authority in primary education' to 'rediscover confidence in our homeland', and teachers should no longer 'be obliged to teach children to understand the past as a source of questioning'. 'To bring doubt on our history: those lessons are shameful!'

For Fillon, the *récit national* was 'the progressive erection of the singular civilisation of France'. This included remembering that 'France had not invented slavery', and that 'France is not guilty for having wanted to share its culture with the peoples of Africa, Asia, and North America.'[29] Fillon was himself widely ridiculed for suggesting that centuries of exploitative colonialism were 'sharing culture', but he was merely stepping into a current that, rhetorically at least, was already running strongly rightwards.

During recent years of murderous atrocities committed in France in the apparent name of Islam, the Front national has not hesitated to make the *roman national* and the threat of loss of identity a central cause. In December 2015, Marion Maréchal-Le Pen, then leading the polls in major regional elections, declared that 'if French people can be of the Muslim faith, it's on condition solely of bending themselves to the culture and way of life that the Greek and Roman influence, and sixteen centuries of Christianity, have fashioned'. Invoking both a royal and a revolutionary tradition, she continued, 'One who has not thrilled to the coronation-ceremony of Reims and to the Festival of Federation is not truly French.'[30]

Six months before Fillon attacked 'shameful' education, Marine Le Pen spoke in strikingly similar terms during a press conference at Rocamadour, an ancient site of Christian pilgrimage and part of what she had dubbed a 'Tour de France of the forgotten'. Too much education, she insisted, 'consists in drawing the attention of students systematically to the most contestable aspects' of the past – including colonisation. It was, she continued, 'a kind of masochism to present our history as a succession of brutalities and turpitudes, yet the history of France is evidently much richer and more complex than that'. She deplored the 'resolutely negative' way in which colonisation was 'systematically treated', calling for a 'rebalancing' of teaching 'so that children can see its complexity'. Le Pen was nonetheless clear what the outcome of this rebalanced complexity should be: 'to re-learn the history of France. All the history of France, the most positive, the most valorising, so that every French person conscious of the past should be equally proud of it, and so that every French citizen should be an ambassador for it.'[31]

We have already seen how such claims might connect with Le Pen's (and Mélenchon's) defiant rejection of the national guilt of the Vel d'Hiv. Likewise, the deep embedding of national-narrative concepts – the American *roman national* and its ironic Confederate variants – has had terrible repercussions for the public culture of the USA. Few countries in the world have more democratic control over their education system than the USA, not least because the electorates and political establishments of individual states insist on retaining a tight grip on 'their' school systems. This, however, has made school syllabi into a battleground for the ongoing politics of cultural identity.[32] Members of the Texas State Board of Education have in recent years 'pushed for students to be taught that the United States is a Christian nation, attempted to smuggle creationism into the biology curriculum, advocated teaching third graders that taxes and regulation are detrimental, and tried to minimise the role slavery played in causing the Civil War.'[33] Published state standards in 2010 insisted that capitalism be called the 'free enterprise system' and attempted to refer to the Atlantic slave trade only as the 'Atlantic triangular trade'.[34]

The Texas board exercises a significant influence over the US national market for school textbooks because of the disproportionate size of the population it buys for and a history of insisting that only approved textbooks are used in schools.[35] Publishers who invest millions of dollars in meeting these requirements then have a ready-made product to promote to other states. An in-depth investigation in 2014 reported that, in striving to meet the demands laid down by the Texas board for new textbooks in social studies and history, even eminent international publishers like Pearson were distorting history. Textbooks contained systematic over-valuation of the 'Judeo-Christian' heritage of US political structures, and of the supposedly peaceful spread of Christianity compared to Islam in particular. One even suggested that Jews were among the groups venerating Jesus as a prophet. Narratives of conquest and settlement in the Americas, and of the realities of slavery, minimised the violence and exploitation involved, while narratives of modern history emphasised the virtues of the carefully labelled 'free enterprise system' and erased working-class activism. In approaching the Civil War, 'states' rights' as a concept was frequently given undue prominence over the defence of slavery in motivations for secession.[36]

The textbooks that were subsequently adopted demonstrated the problems inherent in confronting historical realities in a partisan political environment. A 2015 history text, for example, acknowledged that slavery had been a 'viciously brutal condition for many', but only after explaining at length how useful it had been:

> The southern colonies' cash crops required a great deal of difficult work to grow and harvest. This meant a large workforce was needed. By the 1700s enslaved Africans, rather than indentured servants, had become the main source of labor. African slaves brought with them knowledge that helped turn the wild environment into profitable farms. Many had previous experience raising cattle and knew the method for clearing brush using fire.

The book contained sixty-three individual exercises in which pupils were asked to imagine 'If You Were There'. The only one from the viewpoint of a slave posed the idea of escape as a dilemma, given that 'Your family is all you have' and your choice is to stay with them or to 'try to flee', implicitly by abandoning them.[37] A geography textbook from the same year included a map of immigration to the USA that seemed to represent the northern two-thirds of the territory as having been peopled primarily by Germans, while the territories of the Confederacy were split between those who defined themselves only as 'Americans' and African-Americans, reported in a caption as arriving as 'workers' via the Atlantic.[38]

None of this is new. As Matt Damon memorably expressed it in the film *Good Will Hunting* in 1997, Howard Zinn's *People's History of the United States* 'will fuckin' knock you on your ass' if US classroom history teaching was all you had experienced.[39] That book, first published in 1980, is in fact little different to any number of more academic left-leaning accounts of the iniquities of a society built on slavery and dispossession and devoted to the most rapacious forms of capitalism. Its iconic stature comes from its isolation as such an account in the wider public sphere. In the mid-1990s, the sociologist James W. Loewen attempted to stir up the discussion with his provocatively titled book *Lies My Teacher Told Me: Everything Your American History Textbook Got Wrong*.[40] Surveying a dozen widely used texts, it reported that a mindlessly conformist heroisation of leading figures and self-satisfied acceptance of national virtues was the norm. A second edition in 2008 could only repeat this critique more emphatically – but the roaring tide of demands for essentially right-wing messages rolls on.

But if this is not new, it is terrible. As US National Public Radio reported in 2015, it confronts conscientious (and of course university-educated) classroom teachers with the need to negotiate their lessons away from the official textbook, because that 'brand-new' volume, placed in front of millions of pupils by public authorities, represents 'an attempt in many instances to whitewash our history, as opposed to exposing students to the reality of things and letting them make decisions for themselves'. Teachers like Samantha Manchac, who made that observation, then face the potential wrath of parents – possibly stirred up by right-wing social media – seeing them as saboteurs and traitors.[41]

At a national level, this has already happened. Starting in the summer of 2014, right-wing outlets including Breitbart News and the National Review Online targeted new national standards drawn up for 'Advanced Placement' teaching of US history – school courses for students with university aspirations. Observations about, for example, the 'rigid racial hierarchy' of eighteenth-century colonial society were stated as evidence of 'a leftist slant on our history' and a denigration of 'knowledge' in itself.[42] Within weeks of first being raised, this had been turned into a full-blown conspiracy theory, running back over a decade to suspiciously international academic conferences with suspiciously foreign participants, producing (through the inevitable tenuous and fabricated connections) a suspiciously 'cosmopolitan' approach to the history of a nation that ought to be exceptional and unique.[43]

The academics who had drawn up these standards initially stood firm, but by early 2015 legislators in Oklahoma, Georgia, Texas, South Carolina, North Carolina and Colorado had already proposed bans on their use in those states, and the Republican National Committee had called on the US Congress to defund the initiative as something that 'emphasises negative aspects of our nation's history while omitting or minimising positive aspects'.[44] The result in the summer of 2015 was capitulation – a new AP US History standard document was drafted, eliminating almost all of the more controversial language. Greeted by conservative voices as 'not just better' but 'flat-out good' and 'much more robust, much more historically accurate', it is, needless to say, much more anodyne, uncritical, and accepting of exceptionalism as an underlying proposition.[45]

As author Michael Conway argued in a 2015 essay, the school history textbook in this system is condemned to perform an impossible task: to cement 'the mistaken idea that the past can be synthesised into a single, standardised chronicle of several hundred pages', completely ignoring the fact that any such chronicle is a product of politics and could be produced in any number of different ways. His argument for a consciously historiographical approach, engaging students with the reality of competing interpretations and the choices of evidence behind them, fell on deaf ears, as it has done in Britain and France.[46] While blatantly partisan intellectual gerrymandering may be absent from the official structures of both nations, their education systems are nonetheless under sharp pressure to turn history to wider purposes, and have been for many decades.

For many people of a certain age, the image of British history teaching through the twentieth century can be summed up in a scene from John Boorman's 1987 film *Hope and Glory*, a lyrical masterpiece about his 1940s boyhood. In a dingy wartime classroom, a stern female teacher strikes a map of the world repeatedly with her pointer: 'Pink! Pink! Pink! What are all the pink bits?' Eliciting finally from a pupil that the British empire covers two-fifths of the world's surface, she sternly declares:

> Yes. Two-fifths, ours. That's what this war is all about. Men are fighting and dying to save all the pink bits for you ungrateful little twerps. Page seventeen, 'The British Empire'...

At which point an air-raid siren interrupts the discourse (and the school will eventually, ecstatically for its pupils, be destroyed by a stray Luftwaffe bomb).[47]

Such moments, self-evidently absurd in Boorman's rendering, actually reflect a long and serious educational engagement with the public function of teaching history. From the first generations of systematic public education, history had been promoted for its civic value. In 1905, the Board of Education, in a document decorously entitled *Suggestions for the consideration of teachers and others concerned in the work of public elementary schools*, had nonetheless been firmly of the view that 'there are strong reasons why an important place should be given to history in the curriculum of every school', and those reasons hinged on the key fact of national citizenship:

> In the first place, all boys and girls in Great Britain have, by the mere fact of birth, certain rights and duties which

some day or other they will exercise, and it is the province of history to trace how those rights and duties arise... from the history lessons they should learn something about their nationality which distinguishes them from the people of other countries.[48]

Twenty-two years later, almost midway between the world wars, the board issued a *Handbook of Suggestions for Teachers*, which continued to project the value of history in the same civic vein:

the teacher must deal principally with what children can understand; with personal character and prowess, adventure, discovery, invention and with the way in which men have lived and worked... and with political or religious conflict only so far as its main issues and results are necessary for an elementary understanding of great changes in national life and of the rights and duties of a citizen today.[49]

More than half a century on from this advice, the 1976 Schools Council History Project made a similar point in the language of a different era: that history 'should enable pupils to understand the world around them and should assist their quest for self-identity'. Although it presented itself self-consciously as a shift in perspective from rote learning – addressing 'the process of history, stressing that history should be viewed as a distinct body of knowledge, requiring the cultivation of precise skills' – the element of civic contemporary engagement remained evident. This project, which went on to influence the GCSE exam syllabi that emerged in the 1980s, 'was also concerned with stressing the variety of history and historical approaches', which set the British historical profession up for a battle royal towards the end of that decade.[50]

Having rolled on largely unspoken through the decades in which Carr, Plumb and others had pontificated about history's vital mission, conflicting assumptions about the necessity for an agreed national historical narrative were brought to the surface in 1987. The government of Prime Minister Margaret Thatcher, supremely self-confident after a third election victory, proposed to empower itself to write a National Curriculum for schools, ending the regime of 'suggestions' that had lasted for almost a century. While this covered all subjects, and aroused a variety of concerns about topics and profile, in the field of history it opened an immediately and violently political argument, and one that has rumbled on intermittently ever since.[51]

History as an academic discipline had of course broadened dramatically in the previous forty years, from the first flourishing of Marxist social history in the 1950s through to the various kinds of women's and gender histories that gathered force from the 1970s. Many of these, along with more thoughtful approaches to questions of identity, especially in multicultural big cities, had made their way into the assumptions of school history teachers and on to exam syllabi. To a Conservative government and its most ardent supporters, such concerns were anathema to their vision of how past, present and future should be connected.

Implicitly and explicitly right-wing views on national identity were put forward as the natural consequence of a properly 'objective' treatment of history. The Centre for Policy Studies, a think-tank set up by the Tory Party, sponsored publication of *History in Peril – May Parents Preserve It*, a book that asserted vigorously that history is 'the past regarded for its own sake, rather than a source of lessons or a prelude to our current affairs' and certainly 'is not the application of general theories to particular questions' – posing the question of what, other than a list of 'facts' assumed unquestioningly to be self-evident, could be taught in such a framework.[52]

The element of overt culture war that this debate opened was made clear in further press reporting about particular incidents. In August 1988, the *Sunday Telegraph* reported that 'a dismayed constituent' of a Tory MP had passed him a GCSE paper in which the virtues of British rule in India were called into question through a primary-source extract. Brushing aside the exam-board spokesman's plaintive observation that of course it was a 'biased' source and that 'the examiner was looking for someone who questions the assumptions made', the newspaper reached out to two notable right-wing academics who obligingly commented on the 'kind of Left-wing book club view of history' on display, and countered that 'The British gave India 200 years of peace after 500 years of civil war. That's something else.' The MP who had started this hare running was allowed to close out the piece with his own anxieties: 'Is this how we want our children to be taught? We are not talking about degree students or even A-level ones. We are talking about exams that are the norms for all children aged 15 or 16.'[53]

What the country had embarked on was an entirely political dispute about what children should be told about a single national narrative – a *roman national* in all but name. The right-wingers set out with the very clear assumption that history was something to be inculcated, rather than examined critically; if they themselves did not insist on a positive national story, left-wingers would inevitably indoctrinate the rising generation with a negative one. This stood out even more clearly in a *Daily Mail* report from January 1989, which opened with the stark claim that 'History teachers are undermining children's knowledge and respect for our heritage' and replacing 'Knowledge of historical events and their significance' with '"bogus" skills of empathy'.

The view that 'children are being indoctrinated into assessing the past along Left-wing lines' was asserted directly, along with the claim that 'Any suggestion that the study of history ought to be an enriching experience brings on a fit of the shudders in the average history teacher.'[54] It is difficult to grasp what could actually be meant here by 'an enriching experience', except, presumably, something that would reinforce an unreflective fuzzy glow about being 'British' – at least, for those pupils who would not have obvious difficulties identifying themselves with the victors of Agincourt or Trafalgar.

After all this sound and fury, nobody who has ever witnessed academic or educational policy-making will be surprised to learn that the final report on the new History National Curriculum was 205 pages long and a worthy, wordy fudge. The new curriculum was stuffed with both chronological detail and interpretive oppor-tunities, along with a profusion of optional paths to lead pupils to the brink of what would remain a variety of

GCSE syllabi from competing exam boards.[55] Bloated and ultimately unteachable, it was slimmed down a few years later and squeezed again at the end of the century to make room for urgent emphasis on basic literacy and numeracy.[56] This twice-revised curriculum, now under New Labour management, nevertheless also found space to re-emphasise history's civic role. A leaflet produced by the Qualifications and Curriculum Authority in 2001 promoted the significant role of 'History in the Citizenship Curriculum':

- pupils learn how the past influences the present, what past societies were like, how these societies organised their politics, and what beliefs and cultures influenced people's actions;
- pupils see the diversity of human experience, and understand more about themselves as individuals and members of society;
- what pupils learn can influence their decisions about personal choices, attitudes and values;
- pupils develop skills that are prized in adult life, such as evaluating evidence and arguing for a point of view.[57]

In general outline, if not in implied content, this is the vision of 1905 reborn, civic education for national duties. The leaflet linked issues such as 'The legal and human rights and responsibilities underpinning society' and 'The diversity of national, regional, religious and ethnic identities in the United Kingdom and the need for mutual respect and understanding' to historical topics from medieval law to Nazi persecutions.

Created after a decade of politicised strife, this curriculum itself survived barely more than a decade before a renewed assault, again led by a Conservative government determined to restore the sense of a great national story to history-teaching. Even the fiery Stalinist Seumas Milne in the *Guardian*, while roundly denouncing Education Secretary Michael Gove's apparent desire to rehabilitate the British empire, declared that the previous version of the curriculum was a mess: 'The delivery of disconnected gobbets, the fixation on Nazi Germany and the Tudors, the practical exclusion of vital swaths of history including empire, and the lack of any long-term narrative are certainly an obstacle to understanding the modern world.'[58]

The country thus squared up for another round of 'What history teachers are doing wrong'. A few months later, Simon Schama, appointed to Gove's star-studded advisory panel on the new curriculum, hymned the potential of a new narrative approach to a globalised British history:

Explain how it came to be that in the 18th century Britain, a newly but bloodily united kingdom, came somehow to lose most of America but acquire an Indian empire, to engross a fortune on the backs of slaves but then lead the world in the abolition of the trade in humans; explain all that, and a classroom of pupils whose grandparents may have been born in Mumbai or Kingston will grasp what it means to be British today, just as easily as a girl whose grandparents hail from Exeter or Aberdeen.[59]

Schama, who in 2016 was to describe the Brexit vote as 'The greatest act of unforced national self-harm yet known in modern history', here imagined a version of a British *roman national* that could (in his view) save a multicultural society from losing sight of what was good about itself.[60] But Schama's vision for history collided brutally with the actual aspirations of Tory ministers. By 2013, no longer on the government panel, he publicly condemned its draft output as 'insulting and offensive', a 'ridiculous shopping list' of subjects at once both 'pedantic and utopian'.[61] He was far from alone in his condemnation, prompting a substantial redrafting process in the summer of 2013.[62]

The final version, published on 11 September that year, and currently in force, expresses in its density and detail the intensity with which politicians (presumably representing, in some sense, the public) want history to deliver something very specific and yet also vastly amorphous. The curriculum states that all pupils should 'know and understand the history of these islands as a coherent, chronological narrative, from the earliest times to the present day: how people's lives have shaped this nation and how Britain has influenced and been influenced by the wider world'. To this they should add similar attention to 'significant aspects of the history of the wider world' and 'a historically grounded understanding of abstract terms' from 'empire' to 'peasantry'. On top of this factual knowledge, they should then add methodological accomplishments: from grasping 'continuity and change, cause and consequence, similarity, difference and significance', to creating 'written narratives and analyses', and knowing 'how evidence is used rigorously to make historical claims', and 'how and why contrasting arguments and interpretations of the past have been constructed'. All this while 'placing their growing knowledge into different contexts: understanding the connections between local, regional, national and international history; between cultural, economic, military, political, religious and social history; and between short- and long-term timescales'.[63]

This staggering burden of general expectation on the classroom history teacher is joined by the demand to cover a vast array of particular information. Primary-school history literally begins with the Stone Age, and progresses forward, with various digressions into local and personal histories, roughly to the Norman Conquest. Entering secondary education, and still before embarking on a GCSE syllabus, pupils are enjoined to study British history from 1066 in detail, in four chunks divided chronologically at 1509, 1745 and 1901 – the latter along with a compulsory Holocaust study, some local history, a return to a pre-1066 theme for a further study, and 'at least one study of a significant society or issue in world history and its interconnections with other world developments' that could embrace early-modern India, China or the USA.

What does all of this tell us, apart from the fact that almost all the history of our nearest European neighbours appears to have fallen down a hole labelled 'Holocaust'? The overwhelming message, from this detailed, almost obsessive focus on what, exactly, millions of children should be obliged to learn about the past, is that there continues to be tremendous political mileage, in a divided and anxious nation, in promoting the idea that a certain kind of historical 'knowledge' can save us, and the fear that the wrong kind of knowledge, or no knowledge at all, will lead us to doom. In a sense, this is the same anxiety about readiness for 'certain rights and duties' that has underpinned the aspirations for history-teaching since 1905, but now ramped up to unprecedented heights by the dread prospect of actual decline.

In this context, one of the real problems was exposed in a 2009 group interview with several history teachers. At different points they all indicated that, throughout the varying length of their careers, rote memorisation of facts by pupils has been a constant, if lamentable, recourse when dealing with the pressures of time and classroom management.[64] Grand pronouncements about the value of an in-depth engagement with history (or any other subject) collide regularly with the facts of limited attention spans, overcrowded rooms and constant testing. An academic study in 2016 reported that, despite the rolling thunder of political rhetoric, most schools were successfully giving time to British history and wider histories, including reasonably balanced treatments of imperialism. The real challenge they faced, according to the author, was doing all this 'with often only one lesson a week, and with pupils able to drop history at the age of 13'.[65] Wishing for history to save us, and making the space for children to study it properly, are two different things.

Debate about the teaching of history in France has followed a course both different and similar to Britain. There was never any question of worrying about the government intervening in the school curriculum, because it has been taken for granted since the nineteenth century that it was the government's job to do exactly that. School history curricula, like those of every other subject, are set and periodically revised by ministerial decree, and at higher levels state-run competitive exams for teaching qualifications (the CAPES and *Agrégation*) dictate the content of courses that ambitious researchers have to cram for.

What exactly that content was, however, has been increasingly controversial. By the late 1970s, politicians and professionals alike had, for different reasons, warned of the problems faced by history-teaching – a 'national history sold off to benefit science and technology' in the contest for curriculum space, the 'historical illiteracy of pupils' and the 'crumbling' of history. Left and right squabbled, as in Britain, over how far history-teaching should centre on a traditional model of excellence, 'events, chronology, national history, great men', and how far it should be opened up to 'civic redefinition', but the contest was eminently political.[66]

A few years before British Tories embarked on their National Curriculum crusade, the socialist Mitterrand government opened a political can of worms by decreeing that contemporary history, 'From the Second World War to Our Times', should form a key component of *terminale*, the final year of secondary education. Textbook publishers went to work, producing twelve different *manuels scolaires* for the 1983 season, written collectively by no fewer than 111 authors, around one-third of whom were university teachers.[67] The attempt of scholars to follow the government's instructions around issues – the legacy of Vichy, the Algerian War – where social wounds were still raw, or indeed gaping, produced a fierce backlash. The conservative press denounced the whole syllabus as 'crypto-Marxism', the more centrist *Le Monde* ran a feature intensely scrutinising the 'line' taken by the various publishers, and the widely read magazine *l'Histoire* commissioned an investigation by the journalist and biographer Pierre Assouline that was headlined 'Must we burn the history textbooks?'[68]

In more recent years, as we have seen, loud claims have been made about how dangerous certain kinds of school history-teaching are, and how fragile the hold of the French nation on its precious *roman national* might be. Given the vigour of these claims, the official Ministry of Education instructions on teaching history in French schools are a revelation. The current 2015 edition spells out the history curriculum from when it emerges as a separate subject during Cycle 3, covering three years roughly from ages nine to twelve. Taught as part of the typically French combined diet of *Histoire-géographie*, it is nonetheless also a clear long-term chronological story with highly directed moral significance. Starting with prehistoric traces and rapidly moving to the culture of the Gauls, and the impact of the Romans, instructions on the pedagogic value of this material as part of a long-term *récit national* are specific: 'The history of the Roman colonisation of the Gauls must not obscure the fact that the Gaulish civilisation, of which material traces remain, did not experience a sudden rupture.' The arrival of the first Frankish kings a few centuries later is likewise an opportunity to show 'the continuity between the Roman and Merovingian worlds', just as Charlemagne's later coronation 'reconstitutes a Roman and Christian empire'.[69]

Study next bounces briskly through all of later-medieval

history 'centred on royal power, its institutions, and the territorial construction of the French kingdom'. As lessons move forward into the age of Louis XIV, they also embrace the 'first French colonial empire... the peopling of which rested notably upon the displacement of Africans reduced to slavery'. This year of study concludes with 'The time of Revolution and Empire'. Here the explicit narrative of state-building continuity joins an equally explicit message of republic-building. The notable 'Key stages' of the events of the 1790s listed are 'the year 1789, abolition of monarchy, proclamation of the First Republic, and execution of the king' – the latter three all falling within five months. Napoleon is then discussed as having 'taken power by force and proclaimed Emperor of the French in 1804, but he conserved some revolutionary gains'.

Much of the rest of this cycle follows a similar trajectory down to the present day. In the following Cycle 4, lasting another three years until pupils are around fifteen, much of the chronology of earlier study is revisited in a series of deeper case studies, though also with clear didactic functions. Thus, in European feudal society up to the fifteenth century, state-building returns to focus: a key injunction is to learn how 'royal government sets down the bases of a modern State, imposing itself progressively in the face of feudal powers, extending its domain and developing a more effective administrative apparatus to control it.' The next theme fortuitously combines the discoveries and inventions of the age of the scientific revolution with the continuing growth of a French royal state, and the one after, opening the second year of the cycle, presents the age of Enlightenment and Revolution as a series of progressions – always bearing in mind the 'link with the slave trade and the growth of slavery in the colonies', but ending that 'one will recall the importance of the great administrative and social reforms introduced by the Revolution and then the Empire'.[70]

The final year of this cycle revisits European experiences from 1914 to 1945, the decolonising Cold War and post-Cold War world, and French social and political history from the 1940s to the 1980s. The tone throughout remains insistently didactic, and the very last component of the course is that 'the study of some examples of the adaptation of legislation to the evolutions of society offers the occasion to understand certain stakes of political debate and the modalities of the exercise of citizenship at the heart of French democracy'.[71] In sum, even under the socialist government in power in 2015, the official French history curriculum had an overt focus on a didactic message of long-term national unity that British Tory politicians would have died for. There is no optionality, no picking and choosing by potentially suspect teachers. Its remarkable weight of emphasis on the benefits of a centralised, rationalistic state replicates – more-or-less consciously – what the national elite have long felt to be the essential virtues of their republican system.

Of course in practice French schools face the same pressures of time and resources on delivery as British teachers do. But the extent to which a curriculum as focused on national unity as this one could become the target of right-wing claims that it taught 'shameful' lack of patriotism betrays the vast distance that opens up between any reasonably honest historical evaluation and nationalist myth-making. What is taken for granted in an academic system – that a national history is an object of critique, like anything else, and such critiques can be expressed from many directions – meets insuperable barriers when trying to address the realities of political life and public demands.

As the French public have lapped up Loràant Deutsch's medieval fairytales of Catholic purity, so the British public – or at least that part of it that buys history books – contentedly browses shelves where medieval royalty and wartime derring-do far outweigh any other topics. When more recent social and political history breaks through to wider attention, it is alarmingly likely to take the form of someone like Dominic Sandbrook. Apart from a prodigious – and to some, suspicious – volume of writing on postwar Britain, Sandbrook also maintains a regular media presence, and a column in the *Daily Mail*, unsurprisingly devoted to denouncing the Labour Party, celebrating the Tories, and waving historical expertise around to explain why presumably left-leaning conventional wisdom is always wrong. On the matter of Brexit, he managed to admit to predicting the wrong result, and then claim credit for having in fact warned of the 'unbridgeable chasm' between Establishment and people, if only he had 're-read some of my own articles for the Mail'.[72] By the end of 2016, he was predicting the collapse of the EU within twelve months, having declared boldly a few weeks earlier that Brexit difficulties were because 'Envy and hatred of the British are at the heart of the French identity', and formed 'the most implacable obstacle to a successful Brexit'.[73]

Meanwhile across the Atlantic, the *New York Times* reports matter-of-factly that 'Far more books have been written about the Civil War than about any other event in American history.' A more acerbic take on that would address how many such books glorify fratricidal conflict and the deaths of almost three-quarters of a million people as a great epoch in a nationalistic historical narrative.[74] In the American public eye, the outstanding historian of the Civil War in the last half-century was Shelby Foote, a honey-voiced Mississippian descendant of slave-owners, who turned from novel-writing to produce an epic three-volume, 1.5 million-word narrative history of the Civil War, finally completed in 1974. Self-consciously intent on producing a work to match the scale of the conflict, Foote also emphasised the nobility of the fighting men, and played down the grim political context. The impact of this Homeric tale of noble warriors was reinforced in the 1980s, when Foote, and his poignant anecdotes, became one of the central on-screen voices of Ken Burns' mammoth television history of the Civil War.[75]

Burns' documentary, remastered and reshown to celebrate its twenty-fifth anniversary in 2015, offers other, more sharply critical voices of the war's context, but Foote's capacity to humanise the combatants stands out for its emotive force.[76] His commitment to the South was demonstrated in a 1997 interview, where he said without hesitation that 'I would fight for the Confederacy today if the circumstances were similar', and that 'emancipation' was a sin 'almost as great' as slavery itself – abandoning the freed population to have 'all the Jim Crow laws and everything else' fall upon them, as if these were acts of God, and not policies of the Southern white elite. He also likened the Ku Klux Klan to the French Resistance, said they 'didn't even have lynchings', and described the causes of the Civil War as 'so nebulous and so diverse' that they could not be pinned down.[77] Foote died in 2005, and was granted a swathe of newspaper obituaries. Even the *Guardian* was obliged to note his massive influence, while observing of his masterwork that 'There has, perhaps, never been a history, even a popular history, so devoid of ideas.'[78]

The popularity of authors like Deutsch, Sandbrook and Foote – men of very different calibre in many different ways, but all wordsmiths who form history into desirably unchallenging packages for certain kinds of audience – is undeniable. It points to a conclusion that the wider historical profession, from schoolteachers to internationally renowned critical scholars, struggles to overcome. People, and especially people from privileged groups, do not want to listen to historians telling them bad things about their treasured identities. They will, indeed, forcefully react against such challenges, when given the political rallying-calls that allow them to do so. In that sense, it must be said, they do not want history. They want what they are increasingly getting: a cosy blanket of half-remembering and convenient forgetting that is cushioning their slide down the slope to full-blown cultural dementia.

Conclusion

F rance, the UK and the USA are all currently veering dangerously close to dramatic decline. There is only so long that a rhetoric of national greatness can conceal the gaps between what politicians, and public, would like reality to be and what it actually has become. Emblematic events and situations continually reinforce the divide. British aspirations to Empire 2.0 collide with Indian refusal to do trade deals as long as the UK restricts visas for Indians, as anti-immigrant sentiment demands. The dramatic revelation that headline figures for immigration may actually be drastically overstated hits the press only days after a UKIP leadership candidate openly suggests a scheme for the repatriation of South Asians from Britain, aspiring to what he calls 'negative net migration' of one million people annually.[1]

The air-conditioner manufacturer that Donald Trump declared he had personally 'saved' just after his election, travelling to the plant to make a grandstanding speech, is still moving to Mexico and making hundreds of layoffs just as the company had planned.[2] As the French electorate almost abandons the political process, and the isolationism of the Front national asserts that greater pride in an essentially French history would revive a sclerotic national economy, the Chinese government proposes to spend $900 billion physically reorienting much of the global economy to face towards East Asia.[3]

As I have tried to show throughout this book, the layering of mythology around history is not something that can be simply and uncontroversially pulled back by the application of expertise. The West's current relationship to the past is not the passive victimhood of an individual dementia sufferer, but rather an actively constructed, jealously guarded toxic refusal to engage with facts that are well-known but emotionally and politically inconvenient, and with other experiences that are devastating to the collective self-regard of huge segments of societies that have no visible desire to come to terms with reality.

In June 2014, the black American writer Ta-Nehisi Coates published a long, detailed piece of historical and political work in the *Atlantic* magazine. Entitled 'The Case for Reparations', it made an extensive, evidence-based argument for why the United States of America really did owe its black population recompense – not only for the slavery that had ended formally in the 1860s, but also for the many layers of continuing abusive exploitation that had been enshrined in law for another century and which continued in practice down to the present day.[4] More than one in eight Americans is black, and they remain held down at the bottom of an economic ladder that is purposefully kept so hard to climb it might as well not have any rungs.

Two months later, Coates found himself in melancholy reflection on how the death of Michael Brown in Ferguson, Missouri was being explained away as something other than a piece of brutally evident police racism, and the savagely militarised response to popular protest as other than an occupation:

> destruction is merely the superlative form of a dominion whose prerogatives include friskings, detainings, beatings, and humiliations. All of this is common to black people. All of this is old for black people. No one is held accountable. The body of Michael Brown was left in the middle of the street for four hours. It cannot be expected that anyone will be held accountable.[5]

Reduced to turning the emblems of surrender into a scornful chant of 'Hands up, don't shoot!', protesters who came together in the Black Lives Matter movement are now branded terrorists, confronted by a national right-wing movement to sanctify the status of the police under the label of 'Blue Lives Matter'.[6] A little more historical awareness is not going to solve this problem.

On 16 June 2016, exactly one week before the Brexit referendum, a man who later said 'My name is death to traitors, freedom for Britain' approached Jo Cox MP outside the library where she was to hold a constituency surgery. He shot her in the head with a small-calibre firearm; and as she lay on the ground, still conscious, he calmly pulled a large knife from a bag and repeatedly stabbed her. Her terrified assistants heard her shout, 'Get away you two, let him hurt me, don't let him hurt you!'

The man moved away, returned, and shot and stabbed her again before calmly walking off.[7]

Twenty-four hours earlier, Leave campaigners cruising up the Thames had hosed Jo Cox's two young children with river water as they took part in a counter-demonstration.[8] A week later, seventeen million people decided that a largely fictional case against monstrous EU bureaucracy, a vague aspiration for control and a strong antipathy to immigration outweighed mountains of factual evidence about economic harm and political isolation, and voted for what many seem to have thought was 'freedom for Britain'. According to in-depth polling, with the exception of Sikhs, no minority ethnic group voted for Brexit. Only 27 per cent of black voters did.[9]

During the following year, Gina Miller, the black woman who had fought for proper legal and parliamentary scrutiny of the Brexit process, found herself the victim of an increasing deluge of physical threats, to the point where she was afraid to leave her home.[10] In the summer of 2017, a whole multi-ethnic community was burned to death in the Grenfell Tower fire, which has already been clearly shown to be the consequence of blithe indifference to their safety from wealthy, white local authorities.[11] A little more historical awareness is not going to solve this problem.

In France in the spring of 2016, what the BBC colourfully called 'the regular left-wing alphabetti-spaghetti' of activism, from students and unionists to grizzled 1968 veterans, came on to the streets to protest. The cause this time was the *loi El Khomri*, named after the employment minister, which threatened to roll back some of the cast-iron protections that fully employed French workers enjoyed.[12] This was something French governments of both left and right had attempted to do for decades, and many on the far-left were confident that it could be blocked again. Government refusal to back down was met with occupation of the Place de la République in Paris by a movement that dubbed itself *Nuit debout* – 'standing all night'.

Taking belated inspiration from the US Occupy movement that had briefly flared in 2011, and the similar *Indignados* of Madrid, this lobby promised to suspend time itself until its demands were met – proclaiming after an initial protest on 31 March that April would not arrive and dating communiqués thereafter 32, 38 March, etc. Those demands rapidly expanded towards a revolutionary redrafting of the French constitution, which was seriously debated for many hours, to the no-doubt deep satisfaction of all involved – an 'all' that rapidly dwindled from thousands to hundreds and then dozens.[13] The government, meanwhile, proceeded to ram through the *loi El Khomri* using emergency parliamentary procedures, and it came into force that August.[14]

Pictures of the *Nuit debout* movement, and the marches that preceded it, show a sea of white faces, the occasional black person standing out as an exception.[15] This is in stark contrast to pictures of events later that summer, after the death of a young black man, Adama Traoré, in police custody.[16] Images of the protests that followed – including, ironically, an already scheduled march under the Black Lives Matter banner – show the multiracial population of the deprived estates of the *banlieue*, often in confrontation with police in full riot gear.[17] While the white protesters of the spring were largely shepherded by police content to play along with their game, anger from the *banlieue* was met with overwhelming force – including the arrest of two of Adama's brothers later that summer.[18]

With the authorities denying wrongdoing, the death faded into the normal background tension, emerging again as context in reports of a piece of brutal police aggression in February 2017, when a young black man was allegedly sodomised with a baton after being seized.[19] The situation left the *Guardian* reporting on 'expert' warnings that these districts 'could erupt with violence again', as if anyone with the slightest awareness did not already know that they were kept in a permanent state of semi-militarised police occupation and chronic unemployment – in part by the very sclerotic labour-market regulations the *loi El Khomri* challenged, though also, of course, by endemic racism.[20] And then came the elections of 2017 and after that, even while Macron was in a polling afterglow, Marine Le Pen still sat as the preferred political leader of 28 per cent of respondents.[21] A little more historical awareness is not going to solve this problem.

Soaring above all this, of course, is the absolutely supreme irony that we are still cantering steadily towards a future world literally devastated by the effect of the climate change we created by building an industrialised civilisation.[22] When one contemplates the damage that has already been done, and the very serious warnings of the horrors that are almost certainly to come, it becomes almost understandable to take refuge in the foggy memories of a comfortingly misunderstood past. But to do that, in these circumstances, would be to turn the metaphor of cultural dementia into a reality, because the only way out of that fog would be the inevitable arrival of death. A little more historical awareness is certainly not going to solve this problem.

And now, at the very end, you will want me to tell you how it might be fixed. But I do not know. I know that most people, in their hearts, are not as selfish and wicked as the systems that surround them encourage them to be; but I know too that selfish wickedness continues to be a prime way of accruing power and imposing your values on others. I know that fear is easy, that hope is all too often false comfort and that nothing is harder than grinding relentless work towards something you don't even know can be achieved. I know also that proclaiming dedication to good causes, and spending most of your time bickering and backstabbing, is far too popular a hobby for anyone's good.

Ultimately, I am a historian, not a prophet. I can speak candidly of what has happened in the past and its grim echoes; and like anyone else armed with that knowledge I can see those echoes' continuing impact and their startling, demented new amplification, and I can fear what might yet be. Like anyone else stranded at this moment in time I can only hope that there must be a way to get past this, a way to square Orwell's circle and finally 'throw away the advantages we derive from colonial exploitation' without collapse into conflict and catastrophe. So I turn back to you and ask, what do *you* think that way could be?

Notes

Introduction

1   https://www.unforgettable.org/blog/why-does-dementia-cause-suspicions-delusions-and-paranoia

Chapter 1: Roots of the Present Crisis

1   Full text available at http://orwell.ru/library/articles/European_Unity/english/e_teu

2   https://www.theguardian.com/education/2003/feb/08/highereducation.britishidentity

3   Public data: https://www.google.co.uk/publicdata/explore?ds=d5bncppjof8f9_&met_y=ny_gdp_pcap_cd&idim=country:IND:PAK&hl=en&dl=en#!ctype=l&strail=false&bcs=d&nselm=h&met_y=ny_gdp_pcap_cd&scale_y=lin&ind_y=false&rdim=region&idim=country:IND:GBR&ifdim=region&hl=en_US&dl=en&ind=false

4   Martin Thomas, *Fight or Flight: Britain, France and Their Roads from Empire*, Oxford: OUP, 2014, p. 76.

5   https://www.theguardian.com/books/2017/aug/16/lovers-and-strangers-an-immigrant-history-of-postwar-britain-clair-willis-review

6   http://www.britishfuture.org/articles/windrush-poles

7   BBC report of violence in Nottingham, August 1958: http://news.bbc.co.uk/1/hi/uk/6675793.stm

8   https://en.wikipedia.org/wiki/S%C3%A9tif_and_Guelma_massacre

9   Thomas, *Fight or Flight*, pp. xi–xii.

10 https://en.wikipedia.org/wiki/Maurice_Papon

11 Jodi Burkett, *Constructing Post-Imperial Britain: Britishness, 'Race' and the Radical Left in the 1960s*, Basingstoke, Palgrave: 2013, pp. 21–3.

12 See for example: https://www.foreignpolicyjournal.com/2012/12/18/kennedy-and-macmillan

13 Brief analysis here: https://www.theguardian.com/science/political-science/2013/sep/19/harold-wilson-white-heat-technology-speech, full text available here: http://nottspolitics.org/wp-content/uploads/2013/06/Labours-Plan-for-science.pdf

14 Ibid, p. 1, para. 3.

15 http://news.bbc.co.uk/onthisday/hi/dates/stories/november/27/newsid_4187000/4187714.stm

16 http://news.bbc.co.uk/onthisday/hi/dates/stories/november/19/newsid_3208000/3208396.stm

17 http://www.bbc.co.uk/news/av/uk-17185294/sheds-with-beds-are-london-s-modern-day-slums

18 http://www.historyandpolicy.org/policy-papers/papers/for-gods-sake-act-like-britain-lessons-from-the-1960s-for-british-defence

19 http://www.bbc.co.uk/news/uk-30355953

20 https://www.hrw.org/news/2017/01/12/bahrain-accelerated-repression-jeopardizes-activists. https://www.amnesty.org/en/latest/news/2017/07/bahrain-woman-human-rights-defender-at-high-risk-of-torture-including-sexual-assault

21 http://www.bbc.co.uk/news/world-africa-13881978

22 See this autobiographical reminiscence of growing up in, and out of, such an atmosphere: https://www.theguardian.com/us-news/2017/aug/08/unlearning-the-myth-of-american-innocence

23 https://en.wikipedia.org/wiki/Western_Hemisphere_Institute_for_Security_Cooperation#Graduates_of_the_School_of_the_Americas

24 https://en.wikipedia.org/wiki/Iran%E2%80%93Contra_affair

25 http://www.walesonline.co.uk/news/politics/brexit-means-can-reopen-mines-12809927

Chapter 2: Current Follies

1   https://www.politicshome.com/news/uk/foreign-affairs/brexit/news/87772/customs-union-membership-after-brexit-disaster-shadow

2   http://www.huffingtonpost.co.uk/entry/liam-fox-bbc-brexit_uk_
    5974be89e4b0e79ec199df34, https://www.theguardian.com/
    politics/2017/jun/24/andrea-leadsom-patriotic-brexit-coverage-
    newsnight-eu-negotiations

3   See also the resignation of four ministers within weeks of the
    election: https://www.theguardian.com/world/2017/jun/21/
    two-more-macron-allies-quit-french-government-amid-funding-
    inquiry

4   Twenty-four hours after I wrote this, Trump used a speech to the
    Boy Scouts of America to defame Barack Obama and boast, yet
    again, about the scale of his victory. He is also attacking his own
    Attorney General on Twitter. Twenty-four hours later, he used
    Twitter to announce a ban on Trans people in the US military, to the
    apparent surprise of the Department of Defense. By the following
    month, he was threatening war with North Korea, and sympathising
    openly with neo-Nazi demonstrators.

5   See polling data at https://en.wikipedia.org/wiki/Opinion_polling_
    for_the_French_presidential_election,_2017

6   https://en.wikipedia.org/wiki/French_legislative_election,_2017

7   http://uk.businessinsider.com/polls-donald-trump-in-first-place-
    2015-7?r=US&IR=T, https://www.realclearpolitics.com/epolls/
    latest_polls/gop_pres_primary/#

8   http://www.politico.com/story/2016/02/david-duke-trump-219777

9   https://en.wikipedia.org/wiki/United_Kingdom_renegotiation_of_
    European_Union_membership,_2015%E2%80%9316

10 https://www.theguardian.com/commentisfree/2017/aug/26/keir-
    starmer-no-constructive-ambiguity-brexit-cliff-edge-labour-will-
    avoid-transitional-deal

11 https://www.vox.com/2016/6/23/12005814/brexit-eu-referendum-
    immigrants

12 http://www.coe.int/en/web/commissioner/-/afrophobia-europe-
    should-confront-this-legacy-of-colonialism-and-the-slave-trade,
    published 25/7/2017

13 Some examples: http://www.huffingtonpost.com/brian-hawkins/
    the-emerging-populist_b_9478260.html, http://blogs.lse.ac.uk/
    europpblog/2017/04/30/essay-populism-and-the-limits-of-
    neoliberalism-by-william-davies/, https://iasrblog.wordpress.com/
    2017/02/22/neoliberalism-and-populism-a-short-survey-by-
    mahmut-mutman

14 Here is John Harris in the *Guardian* on Brexit polling day: https://
    www.theguardian.com/commentisfree/2016/jun/23/united-kingdom-
    two-nations-political-chasm-left, and again just after Trump's
    election: https://www.theguardian.com/commentisfree/2016/nov/10/
    donald-trump-brexit-us
15 https://www.nytimes.com/2017/02/10/world/europe/bannon-
    vatican-julius-evola-fascism.html?_r=0
16 http://www.huffingtonpost.com/entry/steve-bannon-camp-of-the-
    saints-immigration_us_58b75206e4b0284854b3dc03
17 http://www.politico.eu/article/steve-bannons-french-marine-le-pen-
    front-national-donald-trump-far-right-populism-inspiration
18 http://www.lavoixdunord.fr/109702/article/2017-01-26/marine-le-
    pen-l-hypothese-de-ma-victoire-est-tout-fait-credible

Chapter 3: Shadows of Greatness

1   Cited in Sudipta Sen, *Distant Sovereignty; National Imperialism and
    the Origins of British India*, London: Routledge, 2002, p. 13.
2   http://eh.net/book_reviews/slave-patrols-law-and-violence-in-
    virginia-and-the-carolinas
3   http://www.politico.com/magazine/story/2017/08/13/what-
    happened-in-charlottesville-is-all-too-american-215482
4   https://www.splcenter.org/hatewatch/2016/03/08/no-ku-klux-klan-
    has-never-ever-been-leftist-organization
5   http://press.princeton.edu/titles/10925.html
6   https://twitter.com/KevinMKruse/status/897255950951866368
7   Cited in Edward W. Said, *Orientalism*, London: Penguin, 1978,
    p. 38.
8   http://www.independent.co.uk/news/uk/politics/nigel-farage-
    fascist-nazi-song-gas-them-all-ukip-brexit-schoolfriend-dulwich-
    college-a7185236.html
9   https://www.theguardian.com/world/2016/nov/16/
    chagos-islanders-cannot-return-home-uk-foreign-office-confirms
10 https://www.theguardian.com/news/2016/aug/18/uncovering-
    truth-british-empire-caroline-elkins-mau-mau
11 https://www.theguardian.com/world/2017/mar/21/kenya-mau-mau-
    case-lawyers-contempt-parliament-foreign-office
12 http://www.un.org/en/decolonization/nonselfgovterritories.shtml

13 http://www.nytimes.com/1993/07/18/world/made-usa-hard-labor-pacific-island-special-report-saipan-sweatshops-are-no.html?pagewanted=all

14 https://www.theguardian.com/world/2003/mar/01/usa.globalisation

15 http://www.guampdn.com/story/news/2017/06/13/decolonization-committee-seeks-help-united-nations/391540001/

16 http://www.lemonde.fr/asie-pacifique/article/2011/08/26/nouvelle-caledonie-ou-en-est-le-processus-d-independance_1564084_3216.html

17 http://www.radionz.co.nz/international/pacific-news/330173/macron-for-new-caledonia-to-remain-french

18 http://atlantablackstar.com/2014/09/30/14-african-nations-being-forced-by-france-to-pay-taxes-for-the-benefits-of-colonialism. Compare with https://nsnbc.me/2012/10/12/french-africa-policy-damages-african-and-european-economies

19 An overview from 2010: http://en.rfi.fr/africa/20100216-50-years-later-francafrique-alive-and-well

20 http://foreignpolicy.com/2016/09/07/france-bongo-bongo-party-gabon-scandal-sarkozy-hollande-colonialism

21 http://www.bbc.co.uk/news/world-europe-isle-of-man-24034768, and https://www.theguardian.com/business/2016/apr/12/overseas-territories-spared-from-uk-law-on-company-registers

22 https://www.theguardian.com/news/2016/apr/08/mossack-fonseca-law-firm-hide-money-panama-papers

23 https://www.theguardian.com/world/2011/oct/29/commonwealth-meeting-human-rights-disgrace

24 http://www.canzukinternational.com/about

25 https://twitter.com/andrew_lilico/status/887605600401731584, 19 July 2017. The original comment was based on this poll: https://yougov.co.uk/news/2014/07/26/britain-proud-its-empire

26 https://www.canzuk.co.uk

27 Of those listed under the 'Our Contributors' rubric at https://www.canzuk.co.uk/, James C. Bennett, Roger Kimball, Michael J. Lotus, Iain Murray, John O'Sullivan, and Michael F. Reber are all US-based, though Murray indicates a previous career as a UK civil servant.

28 See the *Observer* review here: https://www.theguardian.com/books/2006/oct/01/historybooks.features which found it frankly appalling, and a more neutral appraisal in *History Today*: http://www.historytoday.com/denis-judd/history-english-speaking-peoples-1900

29 http://www.telegraph.co.uk/news/2016/09/13/canzuk-after-brexit-canada-australia-new-zealand-and-britain-can, see also by Andrew Lilico, for example: http://business.financialpost.com/opinion/in-the-trump-era-the-plan-for-a-canadian-u-k-australia-new-zealand-trade-alliance-is-quickly-catching-on/wcm/28a0869b-dbab-4515-9149-d1e242b1ef20

30 See http://ipolitics.ca/2017/02/24/canzuk-conservatives-and-canada-marching-backward-to-empire/ for a take-down of the limited and marginal responses to the idea.

31 http://www.newstatesman.com/2017/05/aussies-and-kiwis-can-be-us-brexiteers-so-why-are-eu-citizens-them

32 https://medium.com/@dijdowell/sentiments-and-statistics-why-canzuk-wont-fly-7bd0cef28ff

33 Information in this paragraph from the relevant 'Demographics' pages for each country on Wikipedia.

34 https://en.wikipedia.org/wiki/Foreign-born_population_of_the_United_Kingdom

35 https://thedisorderofthings.com/2017/08/14/historicizing-liberalism-and-empire-on-duncan-bells-reordering-the-world

Chapter 4: Toxic Legacies

1   A recent review of an 'instant' book on the insider/outsider crisis in global politics: https://www.theguardian.com/books/2017/jul/12/the-rise-of-the-outsiders-steve-richards-review

2   This article gives an overview: http://onlinelibrary.wiley.com/doi/10.1111/johs.12153/full. See also this more US-based viewpoint: https://www.theatlantic.com/politics/archive/2017/07/advice-for-the-left-on-achieving-a-more-perfect-union/531054/?utm_source=fbia

3   http://www.bbc.co.uk/news/uk-politics-eu-referendum-36471794

4   http://uk.businessinsider.com/labour-must-sound-patriotic-win-next-election-fabians-say-2017-7

5   A useful overview of the statue, and the controversy surrounding it, is here: http://www.oxfordhistory.org.uk/streets/inscriptions/central/rhodes_oriel.html

6   http://www.telegraph.co.uk/news/worldnews/africaandindianocean/southafrica/11525938/Cecil-Rhodes-statue-pulled-down-in-Cape-Town.html

7   http://www.telegraph.co.uk/education/universityeducation/
    12102384/Universities-are-for-thinking-not-protesting.html

8   http://www.newstatesman.com/politics/uk/2015/11/rhodes-must-
    fall-chants-crowd-bringing-down-imperialist-s-statue-won-t-
    change

9   http://www.dailymail.co.uk/news/article-3369612/Mary-Beard-raps-
    zealots-Oxford-Rhodes-row.html

10 https://www.theguardian.com/commentisfree/2015/dec/22/the-
    guardian-view-on-cecil-rhodess-legacy-the-empire-strikes-back-
    good

11 https://www.theguardian.com/education/2016/jan/15/oxford-
    students-cecil-rhodes-statue-removed

12 http://www.telegraph.co.uk/education/universityeducation/
    12128861/Is-this-how-we-treat-our-donors-Read-the-full-Rhodes-
    document-here.html. See also: https://www.theguardian.com/
    education/2016/jan/28/cecil-rhodes-statue-will-not-be-removed--
    oxford-university

13 http://www.independent.co.uk/arts-entertainment/florence-vs-mary-
    the-big-nurse-off-a7100676.html

14 https://www.theguardian.com/commentisfree/2017/apr/14/new-
    feminist-statue-women-suffrage-millicent-fawcett

15 http://www.telegraph.co.uk/news/2017/07/06/margaret-thatcher-
    statue-blocked

16 https://www.theguardian.com/world/2017/apr/29/renamed-and-
    shamed-taking-on-britains-slave-trade-past-from-colston-hall-to-
    penny-lane

17 https://www.bristol247.com/news-and-features/comment/bristol-
    campaign-group-celebrate-colston-rename

18 This passes scrupulously unmentioned on local tourist-information
    sites, such as http://www.visitliverpool.com/explore-the-city/
    top-spots/penny-lane

19 http://www.nytimes.com/1993/12/17/world/nantes-journal-
    unhappily-a-port-confronts-its-past-slave-trade.html

20 http://memorial.nantes.fr/le-memorial-dans-la-ville

21 http://www.spiegel.de/international/europe/nantes-opens-memorial-
    to-slave-trade-a-829447.html

22 http://www.afrika-hamburg.de/rename.html

23 http://rue89bordeaux.com/2014/05/bordeaux-difficile-memoire-
    lesclavage

24 http://www.nytimes.com/2011/01/03/world/europe/03petain.html,
    http://nordpresse.be/derniere-statue-du-marechal-petain-
    deboulonnee-vichy
25 http://www.bbc.co.uk/news/world-us-canada-39697984
26 http://edition.cnn.com/2017/08/23/opinions/where-are-monuments-
    to-confederate-general-longstreet-opinion-holmes/index.html
27 http://pulsegulfcoast.com/2017/05/transcript-of-new-orleans-mayor-
    landrieus-address-on-confederate-monuments
28 https://www.nytimes.com/2017/03/21/opinion/the-unifying-
    american-story.html
29 https://www.theguardian.com/us-news/2017/aug/12/virginia-unite-
    the-right-rally-protest-violence
30 https://www.theguardian.com/us-news/2017/aug/16/baltimore-takes-
    down-confederate-statues-in-middle-of-night?CMP=share_btn_tw
31 See comments by Jean-Yves Camus and Nicolas Lebourg noted
    here: https://www.thenation.com/article/le-pens-long-shadow
32 http://thehistoryinquestion.com/uncategorized/sessions_jennifer_
    14_03_2017
33 https://www.nytimes.com/2017/07/14/world/europe/jean-jacques-
    susini-algeria-independence.html
34 http://thehistoryinquestion.com/uncategorized/sessions_jennifer_
    14_03_2017
35 https://www.theguardian.com/world/2016/aug/28/french-mayors-
    burkini-ban-court-ruling
36 https://www.theguardian.com/world/2016/aug/17/french-pm-
    supports-local-bans-burkinis
37 http://www.lemonde.fr/election-presidentielle-2017/article/2017/
    04/09/pour-marine-le-pen-la-france-n-est-pas-responsable-du-vel-d-
    hiv_5108503_4854003.html#RagMyYjFo3IFq1fl.99
38 https://en.wikipedia.org/wiki/Ren%C3%A9_Bousquet
39 http://www.nytimes.com/1995/07/17/world/chirac-affirms-france-s-
    guilt-in-fate-of-jews.html
40 https://www.theguardian.com/world/2012/jul/22/francois-hollande-
    wartime-roundup-jews
41 http://blogs.lse.ac.uk/europpblog/2017/04/12/the-grey-zone-of-
    vichy-france-understanding-marine-le-pens-latest-comments-on-the-
    second-world-war
42 https://franceintheus.org/spip.php?article8233
43 http://melenchon.fr/2017/07/17/cela-ne-sinvente-pas

Chapter 5: Who Do They Think We Are?

1 I have removed the verbal tics signalled in the original, see p. 363 of the downloadable text here: http://infojur.ufsc.br/aires/arquivos/RushdieSalmanSatanicVerses.pdf

2 https://yougov.co.uk/news/2016/12/16/why-other-half-vote

3 http://uk.businessinsider.com/brexit-poll-finds-majority-want-uk-to-stay-inside-the-single-market-2017-8

4 http://uk.businessinsider.com/yougov-poll-leave-voters-happy-for-relatives-to-lose-jobs-over-brexit-2017-8

5 https://www.jrf.org.uk/report/brexit-vote-explained-poverty-low-skills-and-lack-opportunities

6 https://yougov.co.uk/news/2016/06/27/how-britain-voted/, and: http://lordashcroftpolls.com/2016/06/how-the-united-kingdom-voted-and-why

7 http://www.ukgeographics.co.uk/blog/social-grade-a-b-c1-c2-d-e

8 http://www.bbc.co.uk/news/uk-politics-38762034

9 Here is a media report on the area from the early 1990s, when it already had problems: http://www.independent.co.uk/news/uk/voices-from-the-other-england-away-from-the-riots-what-is-life-like-on-britains-council-estates-1541993.html

10 http://www.natcen.ac.uk/our-research/research/understanding-the-leave-vote

11 Summary of results at: http://www.huffingtonpost.co.uk/entry/why-did-people-vote-for-brexit_uk_5847d0dbe4b0bba967c1807c

12 http://www.migrationobservatory.ox.ac.uk/resources/briefings/uk-public-opinion-toward-migration-determinants-of-attitudes

13 http://www.newstatesman.com/politics/uk/2017/06/free-movement-isnt-free-truth-about-eu-immigration

14 https://www.nytimes.com/2017/07/31/opinion/brexit-european-union-good-news.html?smid=tw-nytopinion&smtyp=cur

15 http://www.telegraph.co.uk/news/2016/06/04/nigel-farage-migrants-could-pose-sex-attack-threat-to-britain

16 https://www.theguardian.com/politics/2016/jun/16/nigel-farage-defends-ukip-breaking-point-poster-queue-of-migrants. See more generally: http://www.huffingtonpost.co.uk/areeq-chowdhury/eu-referendum_b_10431872.html

17 https://www.washingtonpost.com/posteverything/wp/2016/06/22/the-brexit-debate-has-made-britain-more-racist/?utm_

term=.291819a00156. See also: https://www.vox.com/2016/6/23/12005814/brexit-eu-referendum-immigrants

18 http://www.independent.co.uk/news/uk/crime/brexit-hate-crime-racism-immigration-eu-referendum-result-what-it-means-eurospectic-areas-a7165056.html

19 http://www.newyorker.com/news/john-cassidy/what-do-the-brexit-movement-and-donald-trump-have-in-common

20 http://isj.org.uk/why-did-britain-vote-leave

21 http://press.labour.org.uk/post/146518048964/statement-from-jeremy-corbyn

22 http://www.newstatesman.com/politics/staggers/2017/01/no-brexit-vote-wasnt-just-about-immigration

23 https://www.gov.uk/government/uploads/system/uploads/attachment_data/file/517415/treasury_analysis_economic_impact_of_eu_membership_web.pdf. Figures on pp. 7–8.

24 https://www.ft.com/content/3be49734-29cb-11e6-83e4-abc22d5d108c

25 http://www.independent.co.uk/news/uk/politics/brexit-latest-news-michael-gove-nhs-claim-350m-twitter-vote-leave-eu-uk-a7498651.html

26 http://www.euronews.com/2017/02/09/what-do-we-know-about-marine-le-pen-s-policies

27 http://www.france24.com/en/20170424-france-presidential-election-youth-vote-melenchon-le-pen. See further statistical analysis here: http://www.reuters.com/article/us-france-election-data-analysis-idUSKBN17R1TA

28 https://www.franceculture.fr/politique/age-diplome-revenus-qui-vote-macron-qui-vote-le-pen

29 http://www.aljazeera.com/indepth/features/2017/04/le-pen-support-young-voters-170415161404170.html

30 http://www.huffingtonpost.com/entry/france-far-right-youth-voters_us_58f4dea7e4b0bb9638e5394e.

31 https://jean-jaures.org/nos-productions/le-front-de-demain

32 http://love.hornetapp.com/blog/2017/5/3/gay-men-under-30-are-more-likely-to-vote-for-marine-le-pen-than-older-ones

33 https://www.vox.com/world/2017/5/5/15542242/marine-le-pen-french-elections-gay-outreach

34 http://www.bbc.co.uk/newsbeat/article/39641822/why-gay-french-men-are-voting-far-right

35   http://www.bbc.co.uk/news/world-europe-39433483
36   http://www.aljazeera.com/indepth/features/2017/04/le-pen-support-young-voters-170415161404170.html
37   http://foreignpolicy.com/2016/10/07/marine-le-pens-youth-brigade-national-front-young-voters-france
38   https://www.nytimes.com/2017/02/28/world/europe/france-albi-french-towns-fading.html
39   http://www.newsweek.com/homegrown-terrorism-rising-threat-right-wing-extremism-619724
40   https://www.adl.org/news/press-releases/us-anti-semitic-incidents-spike-86-percent-so-far-in-2017
41   https://www.vox.com/polyarchy/2016/8/30/12697920/race-dividing-american-politics
42   http://mst.michaeltesler.com/uploads/jop_rr_full.pdf
43   http://www.politico.com/magazine/story/2016/08/immigration-1965-law-donald-trump-gop-214179
44   https://www.vox.com/polyarchy/2016/8/30/12697920/race-dividing-american-politics
45   For a strong 2016 argument against this line, see: https://www.vox.com/policy-and-politics/2016/10/15/13286498/donald-trump-voters-race-economic-anxiety
46   https://www.washingtonpost.com/news/made-by-history/wp/2017/08/14/well-educated-elites-are-no-strangers-to-white-supremacy
47   https://fivethirtyeight.com/features/the-mythology-of-trumps-working-class-support
48   https://www.forbes.com/sites/laurashin/2015/03/26/the-racial-wealth-gap-why-a-typical-white-household-has-16-times-the-wealth-of-a-black-one/#4da4f33c1f45
49   https://www.theguardian.com/us-news/2016/sep/20/wage-gap-black-white-americans
50   https://www.washingtonpost.com/news/the-fix/wp/2017/08/02/discrimination-against-whites-was-a-core-concern-of-trumps-base/?utm_term=.fe67c63aedf5
51   http://ideas.time.com/2013/06/17/affirmative-action-has-helped-white-women-more-than-anyone
52   http://www.people-press.org/2016/12/08/3-political-values-government-regulation-environment-immigration-race-views-of-islam
53   https://www.nytimes.com/2017/08/01/us/politics/trump-affirmative-action-universities.html

54 http://www.newyorker.com/news/news-desk/in-trumps-world-
    whites-are-the-only-disadvantaged-class, http://www.esquire.com/
    news-politics/news/a56807/white-affirmative-action
55 https://en.wikipedia.org/wiki/Association_of_Community_
    Organizations_for_Reform_Now
56 https://www.theatlantic.com/politics/archive/2017/08/poll-
    republicans/536472
57 https://www.brennancenter.org/issues/voter-fraud
58 https://www.aclu.org/issues/voting-rights/fighting-voter-suppression
59 https://www.washingtonpost.com/news/monkey-cage/wp/2017/08/
    03/resentful-white-people-propelled-trump-to-the-white-house-and-
    he-is-rewarding-their-loyalty/?utm_term=.33c1e00bd650
60 http://www.huffingtonpost.com/walaa-chahine/labeling-blm-as-a-
    terrori_b_10931812.html
61 https://www.theatlantic.com/politics/archive/2016/10/what-will-
    happen-to-the-trump-die-hards/504032
62 http://www.salon.com/2017/03/25/a-tale-of-two-countries-chris-
    hayes-a-colony-in-a-nation-describes-the-conditions-for-a-second-
    american-revolution
63 https://www.theguardian.com/us-news/2017/jul/31/american-
    renaissance-conference-white-identity

Chapter 6: What Is the Past For?

1   https://www.theguardian.com/books/2017/aug/11/reformation-
    2017-christopher-kissane-history?CMP=share_btn_tw
2   http://www.historyandpolicy.org/about-us/what-we-do
3   https://www.opendemocracy.net/uk/akala/
    battle-of-britishness-in-age-of-brexit-akala-talks-to-convention
4   Ludmilla Jordanova, *History in Practice*, London: Arnold, 2000,
    p. 200.
5   Ibid, pp. 204–7.
6   Ludmilla Jordanova, *History in Practice*, 2nd ed. London: Hodder,
    2006 [reprint, Bloomsbury, 2010], citation p. 175.
7   Ibid, pp. 191–2.
8   Ibid, p. 195.
9   http://www.hist.cam.ac.uk/prospective-undergrads/virtual-
    classroom/secondary-source-exercises/sources-facts
10 E. H. Carr, *What is History?* 2nd ed., London: Penguin, 1987, p. 132.

11 Perhaps unsurprisingly, the robustly contrarian magazine *Spiked* chose to laud Carr for these qualities in the summer of 2017: http://www.spiked-online.com/spiked-review/article/eh-carrs-sense-of-history#

12 Carr, *What is History?*, pp. 155, 156.

13 J. H. Plumb, *The Death of the Past*, London: History Book Club, 1969, pp. 14, 16.

14 Plumb, *Death*, pp. 136, 137, 141–2.

15 Ferguson thoughtfully archives all his journalism on his own website: http://www.niallferguson.com/journalism/politics/ brexits-happy-morons-dont-give-a-damn-about-the-costs-of-leaving and http://www.niallferguson.com/journalism/politics/ no-mountains-flattened-no-elites-toppled-but-brexit-will-still-hurt

16 http://www.niallferguson.com/journalism/politics/sorry-i-was-wrong-to-fight-brexit-to-keep-my-friends-in-no-10-and-no-11

17 http://www.niallferguson.com/journalism/politics/it-is-not-our-finest-hour-but-brexit-must-stand

18 See the BBC interview here: http://www.bbc.co.uk/news/av/uk-politics-36686522/david-starkey-david-cameron-and-tony-blair-s-legacies and the summary of the *Today* appearance here: https:// upsum.news/questions/58db8c57533d6b009ea225c1

19 http://www.patroncapital.com/media/119311/ invitationdavidstarkey.pdf

20 https://www.theguardian.com/culture/2015/nov/19/cambridge-university-drops-david-starkey-video-racism-row

21 For a detailed examination of both earlier and contemporary French 'memory wars', see Pascal Blanchard and Isabelle Veyrat-Masson (eds), *Les guerres de mémoires; La France et son histoire. Enjeux politiques, controverses historiques, stratégies médiatiques*, Paris: La Découverte, 2008.

22 Nicolas Offenstadt, *L'Histoire; un combat au présent*, Paris: Textuel, 2014, p. 7.

23 Ibid, p. 58.

24 See https://fr.wikipedia.org/wiki/Loi_portant_reconnaissance_ de_la_Nation_et_contribution_nationale_en_faveur_des_ Fran%C3%A7ais_rapatri%C3%A9s

25 William Blanc, Aurore Chéry, Christophe Naudin, *Les historiens de garde; de Lorànt Deutsch à Patrick Buisson: la résurgence du roman national*, Paris: Libertalia, 2013, reissued with new afterword 2016.

26 See http://www.theguardian.com/commentisfree/2017/apr/08/
    emmanuel-macron-carries-hope-france

27 http://www.lemonde.fr/election-presidentielle-2017/article/2017/02/
    18/nouvelle-manifestation-de-pieds-noirs-devant-le-meeting-de-
    macron-a-toulon_5081891_4854003.html

28 http://www.jeuneafrique.com/376888/societe/france-emmanuel-
    macron

29 http://www.lexpress.fr/actualite/politique/pour-francois-fillon-la-
    colonisation-visait-a-partager-sa-culture_1825773.html

30 http://www.lexpress.fr/actualite/politique/fn/marion-marechal-le-
    pen-pose-ses-conditions-aux-musulmans-francais_1741502.html

31 http://www.huffingtonpost.fr/2013/02/26/marine-le-pen-contre-
    enseignement-seconde-guerre-mondiale-colonisation_n_2766337.
    html

32 http://www.takepart.com/article/2016/11/29/textbooks-education-
    ground-zero-americas-culture-wars

33 https://www.texasobserver.org/critics-fear-new-law-giving-sboe-
    wide-discretion-textbooks

34 http://voices.washingtonpost.com/answer-sheet/history/the-worst-
    texas-social-studies.html

35 http://www.nybooks.com/articles/2012/06/21/how-texas-inflicts-
    bad-textbooks-on-us

36 https://www.washingtonpost.com/news/answer-sheet/wp/2014/09/
    12/proposed-texas-textbooks-are-inaccurate-biased-and-politicized-
    new-report-finds/?utm_term=.ebfd34408127

37 http://jezebel.com/heres-how-new-texas-public-school-textbooks-
    write-about-1726786557

38 https://www.theatlantic.com/education/archive/2015/10/the-history-
    class-dilemma/411601

39 https://www.youtube.com/watch?v=_2cSB70ZjuM

40 The book has its own Wikipedia page: https://en.wikipedia.org/wiki/
    Lies_My_Teacher_Told_Me

41 http://www.npr.org/sections/ed/2015/07/13/421744763/how-
    textbooks-can-teach-different-versions-of-history

42 http://www.breitbart.com/big-government/2014/05/28/the-college-
    boards-attack-on-american-history

43 http://www.nationalreview.com/corner/386202/how-college-board-
    politicized-us-history-stanley-kurtz

44 https://www.washingtonpost.com/opinions/an-unflattering-history-

lesson/2015/02/19/3be9cboc-b878-11e4-a200-c008a01a6692_story.
html?utm_term=.a07d2657b48d

45 http://www.npr.org/sections/ed/2015/08/05/429361628/the-new-
new-framework-for-ap-u-s-history

46 https://www.theatlantic.com/education/archive/2015/03/the-
problem-with-history-classes/387823/. See also: http://www.npr.org/
sections/ed/2015/07/13/421744763/how-textbooks-can-teach-
different-versions-of-history

47 The classroom scene is here: https://www.youtube.com/
watch?v=6QDIDYXj3Qc and the final scene of the school's
destruction, leading to a 'promise of stolen days', here: https://www.
youtube.com/watch?v=ApTsPrM7XV8

48 Cited in David Sylvester, 'Change and continuity in history teaching
1900–93'. In *Teaching History*, edited by Hilary Bourdillon,
London: Routledge, 1994, pp. 9–10.

49 Ibid, p. 13.

50 Robert Phillips, *History Teaching, Nationhood and the State*,
London: Cassell, 1998, p. 18.

51 It should be noted that, for all its constant debate about 'Britain',
the National Curriculum never applied to the whole UK, and since
devolution at the end of the twentieth century, only applies to England.

52 Edward Vulliamy, '1987 and All That', *The Guardian*, 17 November
1987.

53 Kim Fletcher, 'GCSE history "cocks snook at colonial past"', *Sunday
Telegraph*, 21 August 1988.

54 Stephen Bates, 'History teachers who tamper with the past', *Daily
Mail*, 3 January 1989.

55 Bernard Crick, Review, originally published in *The Political
Quarterly*, Vol. 61, no. 4, October–December 1990; reprinted idem,
Volume 83, Issue s1, September 2012, pp. 394–401.

56 See http://www.educationengland.org.uk/documents/dearing1994/
dearing1994.html#02, and http://news.bbc.co.uk/1/hi/uk/46975.stm

57 Archived copy at www.worldecitizens.net/members/resources/ks3_
subjects/citsubject_hist.doc

58 Seumas Milne, 'This attempt to rehabilitate empire is a recipe for
conflict', *Guardian*, 10 June 2010. Cf. http://www.politico.eu/article/
stalinist-voice-of-labour-seumas-milne-jeremy-corbyn-putin

59 Simon Schama, 'My Vision for History Teaching in Schools',
Guardian, 9 November 2010.

60 See the text of an interview with US NPR, the day after the Brexit vote: https://www.npr.org/2016/06/24/483426383/historian-simon-schama-describes-brexit-vote-as-turning-point-for-britain

61 http://www.telegraph.co.uk/culture/hay-festival/10090287/Hay-Festival-2013-Dont-sign-up-to-Goves-insulting-curriculum-Schama-urges.html

62 https://www.theguardian.com/education/2013/jun/21/michael-gove-history-curriculum

63 https://www.gov.uk/government/publications/national-curriculum-in-england-history-programmes-of-study/national-curriculum-in-england-history-programmes-of-study

64 http://sas-space.sas.ac.uk/3295/#undefined

65 https://www.theguardian.com/world/2016/sep/13/michael-goves-claims-about-history-teaching-are-false-says-research

66 Brigitte Gaïti, 'Les manuels scolaires et la fabrication d'une histoire politique. L'exemple de la IVe République', *Genèses* 2001/3 (44), pp. 50–75; pp. 52–3.

67 Gaïti, 'Les manuels scolaires', pp. 57–8.

68 Gaïti, 'Les manuels scolaires', p. 58.

69 *Bulletin officiel de l'éducation nationale*, bulletin spécial n° 11 du 26 novembre 2015, pp. 175–6.

70 Ibid, pp. 313–5.

71 Ibid, pp. 317–8.

72 http://www.dailymail.co.uk/debate/article-3659119/DOMINIC-SANDBROOK-historian-assure-tumultuous-event-modern-times-people-s-revolt-against-elite-s-brewing-years.html Browse his *Daily Mail* archive at http://www.dailymail.co.uk/columnists/columnist-1057369/Dominic-Sandbrook-Daily-Mail.html. A blog documenting one historian's concerns with Sandbrook's output in detail can be found at https://weneedtotalkaboutdominic.wordpress.com

73 http://www.dailymail.co.uk/news/article-4003794/Why-EU-not-year-DOMINIC-SANDBROOK-political-financial-earthquake-ripping-Europe.html http://www.dailymail.co.uk/debate/article-3984304/Envy-hatred-British-heart-French-identity-DOMINIC-SANDBROOK-secret-Tory-briefing-paper-right-predict-France-bloody-minded-opponent-Brexit.html

74 http://www.nytimes.com/ref/opinion/civilwar-booklist.html

75 http://www.nytimes.com/2005/06/29/books/shelby-foote-historian-and-novelist-dies-at-88.html

76   https://www.washingtonpost.com/news/act-four/wp/2015/09/11/
     how-two-very-different-historians-defined-the-civil-war/?utm_
     term=.6a7a6cf9afe0
77   The interview is linked here, with extensive extracts, and a
     commentary by Ta-Nehisi Coates: https://www.theatlantic.com/
     national/archive/2011/06/the-convenient-suspension-of-disbelief/
     240318
78   https://www.theguardian.com/news/2005/jul/01/guardianobituaries.
     booksobituaries1

Conclusion

1   http://www.newstatesman.com/politics/staggers/2017/07/its-time-
    recognise-truth-trade-deal-india-means-concessions-immigration;
    http://www.telegraph.co.uk/news/2017/08/23/immigration-figures-
    review-new-checks-suggest-numbers-far-lower; https://www.
    thetimes.co.uk/edition/news/pay-british-indians-to-go-home-says-
    ukip-leadership-hopeful-john-rees-evans-f06qvclr7?CMP
2   http://www.newyorker.com/news/news-desk/what-its-like-to-get-
    laid-off-at-the-carrier-plant-trump-said-hed-save
3   https://www.theguardian.com/world/2017/may/12/the-900bn-
    question-what-is-the-belt-and-road-initiative
4   https://www.theatlantic.com/magazine/archive/2014/06/the-case-for-
    reparations/361631
5   https://www.theatlantic.com/national/archive/2014/08/Reparations-
    For-Ferguson/376098
6   https://www.thenation.com/article/case-blue-lives-matter-bills
7   http://www.dailymail.co.uk/news/article-3937642/It-s-m-political-
    activist-Jo-Cox-s-suspected-killer-told-officers-rugby-tackled-ground-
    murdering-Labour-MP.html
8   http://www.dailymail.co.uk/debate/article-3648678/RACHEL-
    JOHNSON-showboating-Jo-serving-country.html
9   http://www.independent.co.uk/news/uk/politics/eu-referendum-
    result-7-graphs-that-explain-how-brexit-won-eu-explained-
    a7101676.html. See a longer-term analysis of polling trends here:
    https://secondreading.uk/elections/brexit-national-identity-and-
    ethnicity-in-the-referendum
10 https://www.theguardian.com/politics/2017/aug/09/gina-miller-afraid-
    to-leave-her-home-after-threats-of-acid-attacks?CMP=share_btn_tw

11 https://www.nytimes.com/2017/06/20/opinion/london-tower-grenfell-fire.html

12 http://www.bbc.co.uk/news/world-europe-35762251

13 https://en.wikipedia.org/wiki/Nuit_debout

14 http://www.bbc.co.uk/news/world-europe-36259120, http://www.liberation.fr/france/2016/08/09/la-loi-travail-a-ete-promulguee_1471176

15 The wikipedia page https://en.wikipedia.org/wiki/Nuit_debout has several high-resolution images which bear this out.

16 http://www.bbc.co.uk/news/world-europe-36854738

17 See the portfolio of high-resolution images at http://rockymattiano.com/clapat_leg_portfolio/the-killing-of-adama-traore

18 http://www.france24.com/en/20161127-young-frenchman-death-raises-concerns-police-brutality

19 http://www.bbc.co.uk/news/world-europe-39011298

20 https://www.theguardian.com/world/2017/feb/14/french-banlieues-violence-theo-affair-paris-police

21 http://www.lepoint.fr/politique/sondage-chute-de-la-popularite-d-emmanuel-macron-et-edouard-philippe-18-07-2017-2144076_20.php

22 https://www.washingtonpost.com/news/capital-weather-gang/wp/2017/08/10/its-unambiguous-and-definitive-five-charts-prove-the-planet-is-steadily-heating-up/?utm_term=.1b724e4b950e

Please visit *http://headofzeus.com/cdnotes* to access
the webpages referenced in these notes.